What are you grateful for?

I Am
Grateful

RECIPES & LIFESTYLE OF
CAFÉ GRATITUDE

Terces Engelhart WITH Orchid

NORTH ATLANTIC BOOKS
BERKELEY, CALIFORNIA

Published by
North Atlantic Books
P.O. Box 12327
Berkeley, California 94712

Cover and book design © Ayelet Maida, A/M Studios
Cover illustration © Frank Riccio
Photographs © Cary Mosier
Printed in Canada

I Am Grateful: Recipes and Lifestyle of Café Gratitude is sponsored by the Society for the Study of Native Arts and Sciences, a nonprofit educational corporation whose goals are to develop an educational and crosscultural perspective linking various scientific, social, and artistic fields; to nurture a holistic view of arts, sciences, humanities, and healing; and to publish and distribute literature on the relationship of mind, body, and nature.

North Atlantic Books' publications are available through most bookstores. For further information, call 800-733-3000 or visit our website at www.northatlanticbooks.com.

Library of Congress Cataloging-in-Publication Data

Engelhart, Terces, 1950–
  I am grateful : recipes and lifestyle of Café Gratitude / by Terces Engelhart.
    p. cm.
  Summary: "Over sixty recipes—including smoothies, soups, entrees, and desserts—gathered from the popular, Bay Area-based Café Gratitude's organic, live foods menu are accompanied by color photographs, easy-to-follow instructions, and co-owner Terces Engelhart's life philosophy and personal healing path"—Provided by publisher.
  Includes index.
  ISBN-13: 978-1-55643-647-5
  ISBN-10: 1-55643-647-5
  1. Cookery (Natural foods) 2. Café Gratitude (Restaurant) I. Café Gratitude (Restaurant) II. Title.
  TX741.E54 2007
  641.5′63—dc22   2006100095

4 5 6 7 8 9 10 11 12 TRANS 14 13 12 11 10 09 08

*This book is dedicated
to my Mother
and her love of food,
with which she gifted me.*

Our Offerings

I Am Thankful

A Note of Gratitude

I am thankful for so many people who made this book possible. All the healers that brought me back to life, the breath workers, the medicine women, the masseurs, the yogis, and the courageous teens and individuals who shared their stories with me and trusted my vision of healing. May we all, one day, live in alignment with nature.

I am thankful for all the wise and wonderful people who forged the trail of living foods and brought it into focus for others and myself.

I am thankful for all the amazing and talented beings at Café Gratitude who crafted recipes and explored unknown territory in creating some of the most flavorful, delicious, stunningly beautiful, and nutritious food the planet has to offer.

I am thankful for Matthew Rogers and Tiziana Alipo Tamborra for their innovative development and mastery of our desserts.

I am thankful for all our managers who dedicate their lives to bringing our vision to life on a daily basis.

I am thankful for Megan Brien who creates the chaos of our lives as the miracle of creation moment to moment.

I am thankful for Cary, my son, and his incredible eye for capturing on film the delicacy and beauty of our food.

I am thankful for Molly, my daughter, and her willingness and dedication to carefully edit every word of this book.

I am thankful for Matthew, my eldest son, and his beautiful wife Syama, and our granddaughter Seyla for their early dedication to the birthing of Café Gratitude.

I am thankful for Matthew, my husband, best friend, and lover, for his vision and passion in being love courageously expressed in the world.

I am thankful for Stephanie Sue Brendle and her commitment to sharing with others the nutritional value of a plant-based diet.

I am thankful for all our generous customers who tested our recipes—your input was invaluable. As we promised, here are your names: Barton, Sarah and Alan Di Vittorio, Greg DeBernard, Chaya-Ryuka Diehl, Jami DeBernard, Michael and Kelly Barrett, Christina Lowe Sullivan, Ralph Helm, Gregory De Hart, Tamu Mosley, Kimberly Call, Dr. Michelle Craft, Ralph Nelson, Sawako Suzuki, Amara Tabor-Smith, Lily, Alana, Eve, Briksha, Torryne Choate, Merrilee Olson-Axtell, Autumn Dawn, Tray Schlarb, Kelly Bordin, Dylan Berkey, Alexandra Wexler, Elizabeth Ferguson, Jennifer Hoban, San-

Orchid

dra Knight, Titilayo Makini, Nkosazana Nkulaleko, Katherine Marie, Patricia K. Johnson, Fuson Wang, Lori S. Wu, Rie Sakurai, John Ashley, Julie Paulson, Arlene Haskins, Ben Wallace, Mary Ann Nelson, Shannon Schafer, Francesca Saveri, Michelle Meeker, Elaine Richards, Elizabeth Stein, Davidian Alter, Radha Lewis, Monique Jones, Michael Pruett, E.C., Anna Hale, Toni Samuel, Alex Korsunsicaya, and Danielle Soucek.

I am especially thankful for Orchid, who dedicated his time, passion, and culinary skills to rewriting our recipes into simplified workable portions so that others might enjoy making them as we do. He was a solid, driving force in handling all the details that led to the possibility and completion of this book. It is an honor to work with you.

I love and appreciate you all.

Introduction

Serving food is a sacred act for me, and serving the best food the planet has to offer is a privilege and honor. Sharing my view with others, along with the healing power of organic living cuisine, is a great opportunity that I gladly embrace. I was taught to love food, and that love affair has been a life-long journey of personal healing for me, so I share my healing as well, in hopes that others might find the courage to embark on their own healing path.

Terces and her mother Leona Lane

Our recipes are simple and flavorful and can be made at home, supporting you in eating and serving healthier foods that provide you with more energy and clarity.

Café Gratitude is our way of giving back; we want people to be empowered in life to make choices that support the planet and ourselves. A conscious, sustainable diet is a big part of that choice.

When we first opened our doors at Café Gratitude, customers started asking us for a recipe book, and over the past couple of years we have thought about all the forms this book could take. We knew that in addition to sharing some favorite dishes, we wanted the book to include highlights from my personal story of healing from food addiction, perhaps inspiring others to heal themselves. And we decided that the book should feature the main focal points of our company's culture, along with—of course—our most popular recipes.

This book is intended to be simple, practical, and inspiring.

Thank you for your interest in sustainability, organic live foods, and in the act of being responsible for what we choose to eat and the impact our choices have on the planet.

We share with you other great books for additional information on an organic live-foods diet in the resource section of this book; we hope you find these as valuable as we did.

— ❀ —

"I've always believed that if people
are given a healthy choice,
they will choose it, and if they
choose it often enough it will soon
be their only choice."

–Terces Engelhart

I Am Trusting

A Word About Recipes and Live Organic Foods

I was taught to cook by following recipes exactly, sometimes measuring ingredients twice, wiping every trace of something out of its measuring cup or spoon. Probably as a reaction to that perfection, I taught myself to prepare food intuitively; my husband calls me a "food alchemist." I might read a recipe through and then simply make up my own expression of it, intuiting what to add a little more or less of. Sometimes I simply get an idea and start from scratch. This is certainly true with living organic foods, especially when wanting to make a version of some old-time favorite that of course is not vegan, let alone raw! The process of creating recipes is excruciating for me—I feel trapped by my own artistic expression. However, I am inspired by the Chinese proverb, "Give a man a fish; you have fed him for today. Teach a man to fish; and you have fed him for a lifetime," and so I persevere and surround myself with incredibly talented people.

What I want to say about preparing living organic foods is that you are working with nature. I call it "kitchen farming," and like the farmer you are creating a sacred connection with the earth and what it produces. No two tomatoes are just alike, some carrots are sweeter than others, what's available seasonally changes, and so preparing and working with live foods requires that you are present; you taste and sometimes adjust for the flavors and textures you are looking to create. This kind of food preparation is an art and you are the artist. It doesn't have to be difficult. Trust yourself. In fact, our favorite dishes are often the simplest. Matthew and I mostly eat foods that are close to the way they occur in nature, only mixing and blending sometimes. Remember, if you start with great foods you don't have to do too much to them.

Entree, salad, and sundae coming off the line at Café Gratitude

Choosing organic is most important. The amount of pesticides and non-organic fertilizers used in farming today is shocking, and it is being ingested by us and the earth and damaging both—for example, conventional strawberries use 300 pounds of synthetic pesticides, herbicides, fertilizer, and fungicides per acre. If you think you cannot afford the extra money that organic foods can cost, consider that we are going to pay somewhere, either up front for high-quality food or in health care for the stress the body endures by having to deal with the toxins we ingest, as well as the health care of all the farm workers and the cleaning up of the environment.

All of our recipes are vegan, which means we don't use animal products. The meat and dairy industries are resource-dense; they require a lot of fossil fuels, water, and other resources. By eating vegan you make more food and resources available for all of us. In recent years the exposure of factory farming and its cruelty to animals has become more apparent; by eating vegan you vote for the ending of this cruelty. You also stop ingesting the violent energy that is held deep within the tissues of these animals. We are becoming more aware that animal foods are not healthy for the human body. We have to transform everything we eat, and animal foods require the most energy to transform, keeping us slow, less alert, and less alive.

There are many great resources for expanding your knowledge and education about the importance of organic, vegan, living foods—see the Resources section of this book. We encourage you to educate yourself and then trust your inner knowing of what is best for you and future generations.

— ❧ —

"Nothing is good or bad
but thinking makes it so."

–William Shakespeare

I Am Responsible,
the Creator of My Experience
A Hero's Journey to Live Foods

I love food. Like all love relationships, mine with food has been a journey. This book is the culmination of my journey, what I bring back and now share with others.

I remember being small, sitting on the counter top in my mother's kitchen as she measured flour and would let me shake the strainer as the flour was gradually sifted through the tight wire weave; tossing the egg yolk back and forth between broken halves of the shell separating white from yolk; turning the handle on the egg beater as I whipped the whites into stiff peaks; pressing the tongs of the fork carefully into the peanut butter cookie mounds to create even crisscrosses. As I write about these moments, my heart opens to my mother's love of cooking and preparing food, which she passed on to me. She is bedridden now and can only occasionally get into her kitchen in a wheelchair, yet still what brings her the most joy is the thinking of, planning for, teaching about, and sharing of food.

My father's jobs in the kitchen involved homemade ice cream (I got to sit on the bucket as he cranked); sourdough dollar-size pancakes, which he taught me to turn only after they had evenly bubbled up; and French toast made a special way he had been taught by the cook on a train ride West as a young man.

My father was a very special man. He was patient, kind, and wise, and he loved sugar. One Father's Day, I bought him an oil drip pan for under his car and filled it with his favorite brown sugar penuche candy; it must have weighed fifty pounds! I kept it under my bed to surprise him as I made batch after batch each day until it was filled. I can still remember going to sleep each night with the smell of caramelized brown sugar filling my room. My mother says he liked sugar so much because his family was poor during the Depression and sugar was a luxury. She made her life about being sure he had plenty of sugar.

My father passed away nearly fourteen years ago, and still there are candy-filled drawers and candy dishes throughout my mother's home.

My sisters and I also learned to set tables, serve courses, polish silver, pour tea and coffee, iron table linens, say grace, and wash dishes. The kitchen was the main room in our family home. My father was a pilot in the Navy so we moved often, and packing the kitchen always took the longest.

When I was sixteen, my love of food turned sour. In an effort to meet my synchronized swim coach's demand to lose weight as we prepared for the possibility of winning the National Championships and then being invited to exhibit at the 1968 Olympics, I started starving myself, eating only lettuce and Tab diet cola. Eventually I did start losing the weight, at the rate of one pound per day, and then I couldn't start eating again. Although I was a self-starter, competitive and strong, my fear of gaining the weight back was too great. We came in second at the Nationals, didn't get invited to Japan, and I was eventually hospitalized at under eighty pounds, placed in a military hospital in the midst of the Vietnam war, molested by my physician, and told to keep it a secret. I learned to lie and fill my pockets with rocks at weigh-in, only to be released into the fearful hands of my mother, who then thought her only job was to feed me so life would return to normal. I finished high school with a tutor and continued on into a twenty-year battle with anorexia and bulimia. Today those illnesses are known and familiar to most of us, though back then I believed I was caught in some unknown swirl of punishment and survival. I majored in Home Economics in college, and my first job was as a dietician's assistant in a hospital. I was married to my high school sweetheart at nineteen years old, when once again I was sexually molested (this time by one of our best friends), and then divorced at twenty. I went on to join the airlines, become a dental assistant when furloughed, work in and around restaurants, marry a Vietnam vet who was an addict, give birth to my first son, move to a farm in Pennsylvania, be hit by my addicted husband, go to work in a local pub, give birth to my daughter, start a wholesale bakery, get divorced, open the first Mexican restaurant in Pennsylvania, marry the bartender who hired me in the pub, become a Navy wife when he joined the Navy, have a son, and be transferred back to the Naval base in California where all of this started.

I became a superstar in a cosmetics company and drove a pink Cadillac. My husband deployed to the Indian Ocean. One day when I was coming out of the bathroom after vomiting, my eight-year-old daughter asked, "Mommy, are you okay?" I brushed her off with a "yes" and then had a sudden realization that I was teaching her to mistrust herself—that she had reason to think I am not okay, and I, who she trusts, was telling her something different. I was not willing to pass that broken and shattered self-trust on.

In the shower that morning, I heard a small voice say, "Tell the truth," and over the following year I started being painfully honest. I cleaned up years of lies and deceit; I broke the twenty-year secret of the abuse; my husband returned from the Indian Ocean, and although we attempted to save our marriage, I was too immature and young in recovery, and the reality of my life-long battle was too incomprehensible for him. We got divorced. For the next several years, my life spiritually unfolded through my dedication to listening to this long forgotten and ignored small voice that continued to teach and show me the way out of the turmoil my life had become. I was taught to face my fears, stay in the moment, and open up to love.

One of the biggest challenges I faced was learning to feed my children and myself. We had developed some bad habits over the years. I could no longer cook the ways I had; I began to awaken to the impact that our eating was having on our bodies and our planet. I went to massage school and started practicing yoga to reconnect with my body and became a vegetarian, reconnecting with the earth. I began to discover that the foods I actually like best are the foods that are good for us: fruits, vegetables, seeds, and nuts. I traveled and worked with teens at risk, sharing my own steps to recovery with others—something I had been told was mine to do by the still-small voice within.

My daughter Molly traveled with me, and we started a small inspi-rational greeting card company to share my insights of recovery and discovery with the world. She was in a severe automobile accident in Colorado, and a couple of months later we returned home. I was reunited with my sons, and for the first time, I was able to go back into the restaurant business and remain healthy while serving.

One night I had a dream where Jesus came to me and asked me to serve at the Last Supper, which deepened my relationship to a life of being of service. I became a tri-athlete and started open-water swim-ming in the San Francisco Bay. I swam from the Bay Bridge to the Golden Gate Bridge, and out and around Alcatraz twice, all without a wetsuit. I made the AIDS Ride from San Francisco to Los Angeles on a bike, rais-ing money for the AIDS Foundation. My greeting card business grew, and my eldest son Matthew and I moved to Sonoma County. My daugh-ter graduated from college and moved to Boston. My youngest son, Cary, finished high school in Coronado while living with his Dad and went on to the University of San Diego. I started participating in trans-formational work, becoming a leader and ultimately going to work for an organization of transformational studies. I met the love of my life while at work one day, and Matthew and I were married in 2002 on a hilltop land preserve in Occidental, California. Although this was my fourth marriage, this was the first time I had ever been married being healthy and conscious. There were two hundred and fifty friends and family members at this inspiring and memorable celebration of love. Matthew had two children in their twenties, so between us we have five amazing and beautiful children. We now have one granddaughter and two more grandbabies on the way.

As I am writing this and looking back on my life, I can see how lis-tening to my inner voice, trusting that internal wisdom and guidance, has taken me step by step through facing my fears and ultimately open-ing up to love. Today, I would say, fear and love cannot occupy the same space, so choose. What is it going to be? Some of you may be reading this while dealing with disordered eating; I encourage you to slow down, go inside, listen to your innermost self, and be courageous enough to follow the guidance you are given. As chaotic and critical as my life was, I recovered myself, so you can too. This is my twentieth year of recovery from twenty years of an eating disorder.

My husband Matthew was the youngest of four children in a family who adopted five other children when the parents, their best friends, were killed in an automobile accident. His parents are both literature academics, and his father taught at the State University of New York in

Matthew and Terces at Café Gratitude in the Mission, San Francisco

Plattsburgh. Matthew's life was given by his spiritual path, which he studied extensively. He grew up in upstate New York, having a much healthier life than I did. When I met him he had been a vegetarian (except for salmon and eggs) since he was eighteen years old. His spiritual viewpoint, connection to the earth, and straightforward conversations continue to be healing. Together as a couple we choose to live our life listening to and following our inner guidance.

Matthew and I were first inspired to invent a board game. This board game, *The Abounding River,* is an explorational board game that introduces people to an unfamiliar view of being abundance. It encompasses training people in a day-to-day practice as well as discovering

a spiritual foundation that opens up to a whole new way of looking at money and resources. We have also written *The Abounding River Personal Logbook* which teaches you about our abundant view of life and offers a 42-day practice in opening up to the unceasing flow of everything. Café Gratitude is what we have created as both a live version of this practice and a blending of the spiritual with the commercial—what we call sacred commerce.

In 2002, Matthew and I were visiting our organic farm in Maui when I read an introduction to living foods. I was immediately inspired and asked Matthew to try it with me for thirty days. He had known about a living foods diet since 1976; however, he considered it to be a last option for people dealing with disease. At this time we were active in yoga and still working each day on developing the game and book. I started reading more about live food and began experimenting with live-food preparation. I fell in love with making food again and reconnected in a new way with my art form of creating flavorful dishes. We started making fresh smoothies every morning and drinking fresh juice each afternoon. We sprouted seeds, soaked nuts, and grew wheatgrass. We laughed at our healthy obsession with food preparation, and I healed at a new level, now being able to once again prepare food for people

I loved, this time knowing that I was giving them the best food the planet had to offer, and so it would be healing for them as well. We thought we would miss our bread, our eggs, and occasional fresh salmon, but we didn't. We came to realize that it was healthy fat we were craving when we thought it was protein. An avocado, a few macadamia nuts, or olives sustained us well.

When the thirty days were up, we felt so good and had so much more energy that we chose to keep going. We joked about really being fanatical when we invested in a dehydrator and turned off the oven for good. I started creating more dishes, more spreads, nut milk ice creams, dehydrated crackers and breads. By now we realized that the Café we were talking about opening was going to serve living organic cuisine! We drove across the country that summer, eating living foods the entire trip. We visited a few live-food restaurants along the way and continued to expand our awareness of what was possible. I wanted to be able to offer the same love and joy of great food that my mother had believed she was offering, only this time I wanted the food I made and served to be healing and empowering. I wanted it to support the awakening of the spirit within, and I wanted the growing and harvesting of it to sustain the planet. That would be a dream come true. Café Gratitude is our dream coming true.

"Pray without ceasing,

in everything give thanks."

–Thessalonians 5:17

Café Gratitude

"What are you grateful for?"

Café Gratitude is not just about great healthy food. Our mission statement says: Café Gratitude is our expression of a World of Plenty. Our food and people are a celebration of our aliveness. We select the finest organic ingredients to honor the Earth and ourselves, as we are one and the same. We support local farmers, sustainable agriculture, and environmentally friendly products. Our food is prepared with love. We invite you to step inside and enjoy being someone who chooses—loving your life, adoring yourself, accepting the world, being generous and grateful every day, and experiencing being provided for. Have fun and enjoy nourishing yourself.

The first part of our statement is about the food and the way it is grown, but let's look at the part that starts as an invitation. We're serious about this—we are truly inviting. In fact we say, "Come on in, try this out, see how you like it" like an experiment. See for yourself how the food tastes, how you feel after eating it, how you enjoy your experience. I encourage you to do the same thing with this book and these recipes. Many people think that preparing living foods is too time-consuming, too difficult to do at home. I want to assure you that it is simply letting go of our scarcity relationship to time that makes this simpler and more fun. Once I started looking ahead and realizing that I was sprouting and soaking today what I was going to prepare and eat tomorrow, I found that I had more time, not less. I enjoy the preparation and the way it is spread out over a couple of days. I began to see it as "kitchen farming."

Just like our view of life and doing business at Café Gratitude is an unfamiliar one to the mainstream population, so is this version of food preparation. Being open to something new can be freeing. Sometimes people feel worse before they feel better; remember, your body is going to start eliminating the toxins that are stored in it when you first introduce whole live foods. It is very important to eat plenty of green foods, chlorophyll-rich vegetables and juices, and go light on the nuts and seeds at first. We invite you to try these recipes, incorporate them into your weekly diet, see how you feel, start taking more responsibility for your health, and start choosing more organic living foods.

The next part of our mission addresses our freedom to choose. When I really began to take responsibility for the choices I had made and was making, I recovered even more of my true Self. Just being *that* every moment is a new choice for most of us. Oh, we may think we have choices but we don't *believe* that every thought is a choice. At Café Gratitude, we encourage our employees to train themselves in choosing their thoughts, choosing ones that empower and inspire them. At first this is often a lesson in humility; it can be hard to believe how many disempowering and uninspiring thoughts we have learned to entertain, to indulge in. Look and see for yourself—what thoughts do you engage in that keep you experiencing yourself as less than? When those thoughts surface, what could you start putting your attention on? This is the kind of work we do at Café Gratitude. If you are going to start taking better care of yourself by eating healthier foods, why not start thinking healthier thoughts? You might already be hearing your mind resist by silently saying some version of "that's hard to do," but consider that a great thought to start with. It's only as difficult as you *think* it is, and you can think anything you want.

Let's try it for a moment: sit comfortably and close your eyes, as sometimes that helps quiet your mind. Take a few deep breaths and then start thinking about all you are grateful for, and notice that the list is infinite. After a few minutes, open your eyes, notice how you feel, what you are present to, and where your attention is now. See, you can direct your thoughts; we all can. We often think our thoughts are automatic, when perhaps they are just practiced and familiar.

The Café Gratitude menu gives you the opportunity to start practicing saying something new and affirming about yourself by simply placing your order. All the items on our menu have self-affirming names like "I Am Adoring," "I Am Loved," or "I Am Fulfilled," which is how we encourage customers to order what they want. Then when the servers bring them their food and drinks, they place them down saying, "You are adoring," "You are loved," or "You are fulfilled"! We've discovered that this isn't easy for people, and we are committed to supporting our customers in starting to express who they truly are, mentally nourishing themselves even before they start eating our healthy food.

Imagine not just visiting but working in an environment that encourages you to choose daily—loving your life, adoring yourself, accepting the world, being generous and grateful, and experiencing being provided for. That's what we provide for our employees and customers. Those six spiritual qualities are woven throughout this book and are also the focus of *The Abounding River* game and logbook practice. Keeping our attention on these qualities is what we believe opens us up to the unceasing flow of everything!

Consider that the greatest way we, who have been blessed with so much, can impact our life on this amazing planet is to start being grateful for all we have already been given!

I am so grateful.

— ❀ —

"When God sends rain,
rain is my choice."

– James W. Riley

I Am Loving and Accepting: Appetizers and Side Dishes

These items can be eaten as appetizers or light snacks—they are all nutritious and can easily be shared. Many can be made ahead of time and then simply assembled when ready to eat.

Being loving and accepting is about letting go of our judgments and opinions. It's about accepting others and life just the way it is and just the way it isn't. Where are you judging someone or something else? Is it in the way of you experiencing being connected or related? What do you think might be available if you gave up or let go of those judgments? Can you see that this practice might just open up a lot more opportunities to sit with others and share a snack or appetizer and enjoy the unique qualities of one another? When you catch yourself making someone wrong or fighting for your rightness, stop and ask yourself, "What would love do now?"

I Am Spirit

TERIYAKI ALMONDS

Makes about 3 cups

2½ cups soaked almonds (see page 153)
⅓ cup well packed, chopped dates
¼ cup Nama Shoyu (see page 153)
1½ teaspoon chopped garlic
1 teaspoon finely minced ginger

Rinse and drain almonds. In your food processor fitted with the "S" blade, purée dates, Nama Shoyu, garlic, and ginger until smooth. Toss the almonds in the paste until well coated.

Have ready one dehydrator tray fitted with both a grid and a Teflex sheet. Place the almond mixture onto the Teflex sheet and spread out into a single layer. Dehydrate at 145° for 1 hour. Turn the dehydrator down to 115° and continue dehydrating until the almonds form a skin, then flip them onto the grid sheet, peeling off the Teflex sheet; continue to dehydrate until dry, about 48 total hours.

What is your word
for Spirit?

I Am Welcoming

ENDIVE BOATS STUFFED WITH MARINATED MUSHROOMS

Makes about 40 hors d'oeuvres

FOR THE MARINADE
1 teaspoon finely chopped jalapeño
1 teaspoon finely chopped ginger
½ teaspoon finely chopped garlic
2 tablespoons Nama Shoyu (see page 153)
2 teaspoons lime juice
1 tablespoon agave nectar

FOR THE MUSHROOM MIXTURE
2 cups shiitake mushrooms, ⅛-inch dice
½ cup daikon, ⅛-inch dice
½ cup sweet pepper, ⅛-inch dice
2 Kaffir lime leaves, shredded (see page 151)

TO FINISH
6 Belgian endives*
1 lime slice
A handful of mesclun mixed greens (optional)

---

* You can use another type of lettuce such as bib or romaine to
create cups, although I think endive makes the best vessel for this.

Place the chopped ingredients for the marinade in a medium bowl and
add the liquid ingredients.

Prepare all the ingredients in the mushroom mixture and toss into the
marinade; let set for at least 1 hour.

To serve, cut off the end of an endive and rub with a little lime. Now pull off several leaves. You may need to cut and rub again as you reach further into the center. (But you'll only want to use the larger of the leaves for this recipe. The centers are great cut up in a salad.) Now scatter some mesclun mixed greens on top of a serving platter. Next stuff about a teaspoon of the marinated mushroom mixture into the bottom portion of each leaf. Arrange them around the edge of the platter. Place a flower or some nice ornament in the center of the plate.

Shiitake mushrooms are known to lower cholesterol, cleanse blood, and contain lenitan, a phytochemical found in dozens of studies to have potent anti-carcinogenic qualities.

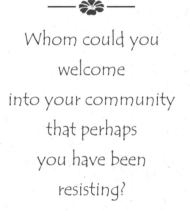

Whom could you
welcome
into your community
that perhaps
you have been
resisting?

I Am Magical

MARINATED MUSHROOM CAPS STUFFED WITH MUSHROOM PÂTÉ

Makes 2 cups pâté

16 crimini mushrooms, stems removed (reserve stems!)

FOR THE MARINADE
2 tablespoons Nama Shoyu (see page 153)
2 tablespoons lemon juice

FOR THE PÂTÉ
1½ cups soaked sunflower seeds (see page 153)
½ cup soaked pecans or walnuts (see page 153)
1 cup mushroom stems
3 green onions, chopped
¼ cup packed cilantro with stems, chopped
1 teaspoon chopped garlic
2 tablespoons Nama Shoyu (see page 153)
¼ teaspoon salt
½ teaspoon freshly ground black pepper

GARNISH
½ cup **I Am Focused** Brazil Nut Parmesan Cheese (see page 56)
A handful of mesclun mixed greens (optional)

Start by wiping clean your mushrooms, being careful not to damage the caps. Remove and save the stems. Place the mushroom caps in a glass bowl with the Nama Shoyu and lemon juice. Stir gently and set aside. Toss every half hour or so. Ideally these will marinate for a few hours.

Now you're ready to make the pâté. In the bowl of a food processor fitted with the "S" blade, purée the chopped green onions, cilantro, garlic, and Nama Shoyu. Add the salt and pepper along with the rinsed and drained seeds and nuts. Purée to a smooth paste. Taste and adjust seasonings if necessary.

Next, stuff the mushrooms. If you have a pastry bag, that will work well to fill the caps. In the restaurant we have a tiny ice cream scoop that pops out a little ball of pâté. In any case, I know you're clever. A small spoon and a finger or two spoons to feed the pâté into the cap will do fine. Once all your caps are stuffed, drizzle a little Nama Shoyu over each one. Then sprinkle with a little **I Am Focused** Brazil Nut Parmesan Cheese.

Serving suggestion: These look especially nice over a bed of mesclun or other greens you may have on hand.

What's one miracle

you've experienced in

your life?

I Am Kind

REFRIED BEANS

Makes just under 2 cups

Presoak the first three ingredients for 4 hours:

¾ dried chipotle chile (reserve water)

8 sun-dried tomato halves (reserve water)

2 cups sunflower seeds (soaked and drained,
   see page 153)

½ jalapeño

2 green onions, chopped

¼ cup packed cilantro with stems, chopped

¼ teaspoon chili powder

½ teaspoon salt

¾ teaspoon cumin powder

¼ cup olive oil

1 teaspoon lemon juice

¼ teaspoon chopped garlic

In the bowl of a food processor fitted with the "S" blade,* purée the drained seeds, tomatoes, and chipotle to a smooth pâté. (Save a few tablespoons of sun seeds to mix in at the end for a chunky texture.) Now place the rest of the ingredients in the bowl of the food processor, and continue to purée until smooth.

It will be necessary to add a little of the reserved water to create a smooth pâté; use the tomato water for this purpose. And if you like it on the spicy side use the chipotle water as well. Be careful not to use too much water. You're looking for a consistency similar to refried beans.

Finally, taste your pâté and adjust the flavor if necessary. When you are satisfied with the flavor, fold in the remaining sunflower seeds. Now your pâté is ready to serve as part of **I Am Honoring** Nachos (see page 10) or to be used in another of our recipes!

Note: This is intended to be spicy!

---

* If you happen to have a Kitchen Aid mixer and the meat grinder attachment, you might want to use it for this recipe. Just process all ingredients (minus the tomato or chipotle water) through it instead of the food processor. Then stir in enough of either tomato or chipotle water to create a consistency similar to refried beans. Fold in the reserved sunflower seeds.

Sunflower seeds are high in protein and rich in essential omega-6 fatty acid, calcium, and iron.

When did someone's
kindness
make a difference
in your life?

I Am Honoring

NACHOS

Serves 4

On an appetizer-size plate, put one large scoop of **I Am Kind** Refried Beans (see page 8). Next to that place another large scoop of **I Am Generous** Guacamole (see page 17). Top both with **I Am Fiery** Salsa Fresca (see page 20), and **I Am Ravishing** Cashew Sour Cream (see page 48). Insert four large pieces of **I Am Relishing** Buckwheat Crackers (see page 62) and serve.

What quality do you
honor in others?

I Am Bountiful

BRUSCHETTA

Serves 4

2 cups diced tomatoes
½ cup chiffonade basil
1 teaspoon smashed garlic
¼ teaspoon salt
½ cup olive oil
4 slices **I Am Fun** Almond Toast (see page 59)
¼ cup **I Am Focused** Brazil Nut Parmesan (see page 56)

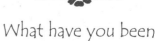

What have you been
generously given?

In a salad mixing bowl toss the above ingredients until well mixed. Place four slices of **I Am Fun** Almond Toast onto serving plate and top with tomato mixture. Sprinkle with **I Am Focused** Brazil Nut Parmesan Cheese and serve.

I Am Happy

ALMOND HUMMUS

Makes 3 cups

2½ cups soaked almonds (see page 153)
¼ cup + 1 tablespoon raw tahini
¾ teaspoon freshly ground black pepper
1½ teaspoon chopped garlic
1¾ teaspoon cumin
¼ cup + 2 tablespoons olive oil
¼ cup + 3 tablespoons lemon juice
¾ cup water
¾ teaspoon salt

In the bowl of a food processor fitted with the "S" blade, grind down the drained and rinsed almonds. Add the remaining ingredients, minus half the water. Begin again to purée the ingredients together, adding water until you reach a creamy texture (or one that you desire).

Taste the hummus and adjust any ingredients to your liking: garlic, lemon juice, cumin, olive oil.

This can be served drizzled with olive oil and dusted with cumin and/or paprika.

Tahini made from whole sesame seeds is high in calcium and makes a great replacement for rich dairy products.

— ❧ —

Can you see that the source of
happiness is being happy?

I Am Present

FARMER-STYLE CHEESE

Makes approximately 1½ cups

1½ cups soaked cashews (see page 153)
1 tablespoon miso
1 pinch salt
1 teaspoon coconut oil
¾ cup fresh water

Place the soaked and rinsed cashews in a blender along with miso, salt, oil, and half the water. Start to blend on low, turning up the speed slowly. Add more water as necessary to keep mixture pulling down to the bottom of the blender. When a smooth consistency has been achieved, taste your creation. This cheese can be used as is or hung in a double layer of moistened cheesecloth to ripen and drain, making a slightly firmer and tangier cheese.

> **Note:** You can change the flavor or color of this cheese very easily by adding one or more of the following: cumin powder, turmeric powder, parsley, cilantro, bell or black pepper. Be inventive and let your creative juices flow! (Just remember if you're going to be using cilantro, parsley, or bell pepper, chop them first and add them from the beginning so they have a chance to be well incorporated.)

I Am Entrusted

PEPPER JACK CHEESE

Makes approximately 1½ cups

2 ounces Irish moss (presoak in 1½ cups water,
    overnight, rinse well)
2 cups soaked cashews (see page 153)
1 tablespoon miso
1 teaspoon salt
1½–2 jalapeño peppers
2 teaspoons unscented coconut oil
¾ cup fresh water

Rinse the soaked Irish moss, cut into small pieces, and place into blender carafe. Add enough water to cover the Irish moss. Blend, starting on low speed and increasing speed as moss emulsifies. Turn off blender and add the soaked and rinsed cashews along with miso, salt, peppers, oil, and half of the water. Start to blend again on low, turning up the speed slowly. Add only enough water to keep mixture blending. When a thick smooth consistency has been achieved, taste your creation, and adjust salt and spice to taste. Scrape cheese into container lined with cheesecloth, fold cheesecloth over cheese, and refrigerate until firm.

Remove cheese from container and unwrap cheesecloth. Turn cheese onto plate and slice into wedges.

> **Serving suggestion:** Serve with **I Am Relishing** Buckwheat Crackers (see page 62) and fresh fruit.

— ❋ —

What is your experience
when you are
completely present
with another person?

I Am Opulent

OLIVE TAPENADE

Makes 1½ cups

¼ cup finely chopped cilantro, with stems
1 teaspoon chopped garlic
½ jalapeño pepper, chopped, with seeds
¼ cup olive oil
1 cup pitted Kalamata olives*
1 cup pitted green olives*

---

* Remember to sift through your olives for stray pits
  before you purée them.

In the bowl of a food processor fitted with the "S" blade, process the
following: chopped cilantro, garlic, and jalapeño, along with olive oil.
Process until smooth and fine. Add the olives and mix to the desired
consistency—slightly chunky or fairly smooth.

— ❀ —

Where does life

exceed

your expectations?

I Am Generous with I Am Fiery Salsa Fresca and I Am Releasing Flax Crackers

I Am Generous

GUACAMOLE

Makes about 2 cups

3 large avocados, mashed (about 2 cups)
2 tablespoons finely chopped cilantro
½ teaspoon chopped jalapeño, with seeds
½ teaspoon salt
1½ tablespoons lime or lemon juice

Fold all of your prepared ingredients into your mashed avocados. Taste and adjust seasonings if necessary.

How could you be more
generous with yourself?

I Am Grateful

MARINATED VEGGIES

Makes 4 cups

Dice or grate 4 cups of the following:
Carrot, celery, radish, zucchini, and fennel bulb*

FOR THE MARINADE
3 tablespoons chopped cilantro with stems
1 teaspoon chopped garlic
1 tablespoon + 1 teaspoon chopped ginger
2 tablespoons olive oil
1 tablespoon Nama Shoyu (see page 153)
2 tablespoons lemon juice
¼ teaspoon salt
⅛ teaspoon cayenne

---

* Feel free to mix and match the veggies you use in this recipe.
  Sunchokes, celery root, broccoli stems, and cauliflower would all be
  great in here, too.

Place all of the marinade ingredients in your blender on high until well
puréed. Pour over your grated veggies and stir well. Ideally, for the most
flavor, marinate for at least 1 hour. These veggies can be used in lots
of recipes.

Share with someone
three things you are
grateful for.

Do you empower and
trust your insights?

I Am Insightful

SPINACH-WRAPPED SAMOSAS (see photograph page 1)

Serves 4–6

3 **I Am Bueno** Spinach Tortillas (see page 66)
1 cup **I Am Happy** Almond Hummus (see page 12)
⅔ cup **I Am Grateful** Marinated Veggies (see page 18)
⅔ cup **I Am Spicy** Jalapeño Mint Chutney (see page 49)

Spread ⅓ cup almond hummus evenly on each of three tortillas. Top with marinated veggies. Fold corners of tortillas into center, making four triangle-shaped pieces. Cut into four triangles and place on small plate with a ramekin of jalapeño mint chutney in the center for dipping.

"In ordinary life we hardly realize
that we receive a great deal more
than we give, and that it is only with
gratitude that life becomes rich.

–Dietrich Bonhoeffe

I Am Fiery

SALSA FRESCA

Makes 3 cups

2 large ripe tomatoes (about 1¼ pounds)
3 tablespoons lime or lemon juice
½ teaspoon chopped garlic
⅓ cup chopped red onion
1 jalapeño pepper
⅓ bunch cilantro with stems, chopped
½ teaspoon salt
1 teaspoon agave nectar (see page 149)

I prefer the flavor and texture of this salsa if all the ingredients are chopped by hand. In this case chop all your ingredients to a small dice and mix together. Let stand at least a few minutes for flavors to meld. Taste and adjust the lime juice, salt, and jalapeño to your liking.

You can turn this salsa into a tropical fiesta by adding one or more of the following fruits: pineapple, kiwi, mango and/or papaya. Substitute measure for measure chopped tropical fruit for tomato.

Spicy foods such as hot chile peppers, garlic, mustard, and horseradish increase overall metabolic activity (fat-calorie burning rate) by 25%.

Who inspires you?

I Am Flourishing Falafels with I Am Happy Almond Hummus and I Am Opulent Olive Tapenade

I Am Flourishing

FALAFELS

Makes about 8–10 falafels

½ cup soaked sesame seeds (see page 153)

1 cup soaked pecans or walnuts (see page 153)

1 cup soaked almonds (see page 153)

¼ cup olive oil

2 tablespoons lemon juice

¼ jalapeño pepper

¼ cup loosely packed parsley leaves

¼ cup loosely packed cilantro leaves

3 cloves garlic

2 teaspoons oregano flakes

1 teaspoon freshly ground black pepper

1½ teaspoons ground cumin

1½ teaspoons salt

¼–½ cup fresh water

First rinse and drain your nuts, then set aside.

Fit your food processor with the "S" blade.* Purée the jalapeño, parsley, cilantro, and garlic with the olive oil and lemon juice. You're looking to create a smooth paste, so scrape down the bowl if necessary to do so. Add your rinsed and drained nuts along with all of the dry spices. Purée until all the nuts are ground to about the size of a sesame seed or smaller. You may need to scrape down the bowl multiple times. Add fresh water if necessary, both to achieve the fine grind and to create a "batter" that will stick together, being careful not to create dough that is too wet to shape into patties or balls.

Have ready one dehydrator tray fitted with a grid sheet. (If your falafel batter got too moist, use a Teflex sheet for the first hour or so and then flip the falafels onto the grid sheet.) Moisten hands with fresh water and form falafel patties three-quarters of an inch thick and one and a half inches across. Place them on the dehydrator sheet. Dehydrate at 145° for 1 hour and then turn temperature down to 115° until dry. If you're going to eat them all at once or don't mind storing them in the fridge, you don't need to dry them completely; about three-quarters of the way will do. If fully dry, they will keep in an airtight container for about a week.

At the cafés we serve the falafels as a Mediterranean plate with **I Am Happy** Almond Hummus (see page 12), **I Am Opulent** Olive Tapenade (see page 16), and **I Am Light** Tzatziki (see page 53).

---

* If you happen to have a Kitchen Aid mixer with the meat grinder attachment, you might want to use it for this recipe, as the texture of the falafel is a little more genuine. Just process all ingredients (minus the liquids) through the Kitchen Aid instead of the food processor. Then add all the lemon juice and water as necessary to create a sticky batter.

Sesame seeds are the most abundant source of calcium known. They have ten times more calcium than cow's milk, one and a half times the amount of iron in beef liver, more protein than chicken or beef, and three times the phosphorus.

What is your
greatest asset?

I Am Flowing

VEGGIE NOODLES

Makes 3 cups raw, serves 1–2

11 ounces celery root (before peeling)

or

10 ounces of the following: parsnip, zucchini, or daikon

Get out your spiralizer and place in the desired blade (the small blade for spaghetti and one of the wider blades for fettucini). Place your peeled root vegetable in, and spiral away.

Toss the noodles with a pinch of salt and a little olive oil to soften.

Dress noodles with your favorite sauce or place in your favorite soup.

Where could you be
more flexible??

I Am Whole-Hearted

RAW VEGGIE RICE

Makes 2 cups "rice"

10 ounces parsnips or celery root (before peeling)
¼ cup pine nuts
1 pinch finely chopped garlic
Salt and white pepper to taste

Peel and grate the celery root. Spread onto a chopping board and cut into shorter, more rice-like segments. Finely chop or mash the garlic and pine nuts almost into a paste. Toss this with the root rice and add salt and pepper to taste. Dehydrate 10–30 minutes at 115° to achieve a softer texture.

You are now ready to serve this up with your favorite **I Am Elated** Enchiladas (see page 69) or rolled up into **I Am Enrolled** Nori Rolls (see page 81), our live sushi!

If you want to create a pilaf, you could add some sage, cinnamon, currants, and anything else that strikes your fancy. Adding the following could make fried rice: a little fresh cilantro, powdered anise, and coriander with a few diced veggies such as carrot, burdock, and sweet pepper.

— ❀ —

When do you feel
most alive?

I Am Grateful:
Soups and Salads

*S*oups are a wonderful light lunch or supper along with a salad. With garnishing they can also become beautiful masterpieces. I prefer our soups slightly warmed by blending them at the time of serving. Like juices, these soups are nutrient-dense, and a little soup can be very nourishing.

When it comes to salads, the possible creations are infinite. We share in these pages our customers' favorites. Salad dressings are also a wonderful way to experiment with flavors and herbs and to add nutrition and substance to salad greens.

When we first started sharing our thoughts and ideas about live foods with our family and friends, they thought we meant carrot and celery sticks, probably with ranch dressing. We often giggle about that now. The world of fruits and vegetables is expansive and fun to explore. Start going to any local farmers' markets in your area and see what's available. Ask the vendors questions about their farms and the produce they grow—they love to share their passion with you.

Any time you notice yourself stopped in your practice of keeping your attention on qualities that inspire you, or suddenly realize that your thoughts are entertaining some version of "something's wrong," or "life shouldn't be this way," or you are saying "should" and "have to" quite often, simply shift your attention to what you are grateful for or maybe ask someone you are with what they are grateful for. Gratitude expands our experience; it gets us out of our small little self and connects us with the universe.

When we were working on opening the first Café Gratitude, we started asking everyone we met each day what they were grateful for. Some of the most suppressed office environments came to life, as people said things like "No one has ever asked me that question before!" and "Imagine what City Hall would be like if we asked each other that question every morning!" Try it! See what happens in your family, workplace, or community. Watch how the conversations shift and start connecting you. What are you grateful for?

I Am Divine

FIERY CARROT AVOCADO SOUP (see photograph page 25)

Makes 3 cups, serves 3–4

2 cups carrot juice
1 large avocado (save a bit for the garnish)
1 tablespoon + 1 teaspoon minced ginger
1 tablespoon + 1 teaspoon lemon juice
½ jalapeño pepper
½ teaspoon chopped garlic
¼ teaspoon cayenne pepper
5 mint leaves
15 large basil leaves
1 tablespoon + 1 teaspoon olive oil

Place all ingredients in your blender. Purée until smooth. Taste and adjust seasonings if necessary.

Pour into three or four bowls, and garnish with a mint leaf or a thin slice of avocado.

Note: To gently warm this soup, simply blend a little longer. The friction alone will create heat.

Capsaicin in chile peppers such as cayenne and habanero provides anti-inflammatory and anti-carcinogenic benefits.

How do you connect
to the Divine?
Who do you serve?

——— ❀ ———

Who could you thank
that perhaps you haven't
thanked before?

I Am Thankful

COCONUT CURRY SOUP

Serves 4

4 cups coconut milk (see page 91)
2 tablespoons minced ginger
1 teaspoon garlic
2 tablespoons lemon juice
¼ cup olive oil
1 tablespoon large date, chopped
½ teaspoon salt
1 tablespoon Nama Shoyu (see page 153)
1 tablespoon + 1 teaspoon East Indian curry powder
1 jalapeño pepper

FOR THE GARNISH
1 avocado, cubed
⅓ cup diced tomato
⅓ cup diced cucumber
½ cup marinated shiitake mushrooms (see page 155)
¼ cup cilantro leaves

Add all but the garnish ingredients to the blender and purée until smooth. You should have a nice rich golden soup. Taste your soup and adjust the flavors: sweet, spicy, and salty as necessary. Some coconuts can be sweeter than others. Jalapeños can also vary greatly in heat.

When the soup base is to your liking, divide among four bowls. Add the garnish ingredients and top with a few cilantro leaves.

I Am Adventurous

THOM KA, A TRADITIONAL THAI SOUP

Serves 2 as a main course or 4 as a soup course

FOR THE SOUP BASE

3 cups coconut milk (see page 91)

¼ cup Nama Shoyu (see page 153)

3 tablespoons lime juice

2 tablespoons agave nectar

2 stalks lemongrass (see page 152)

1 inch fresh ginger

1 teaspoon minced jalapeño

½ teaspoon chopped garlic

VEGGIES FOR THE SOUP

⅔ cup shredded kale or purple cabbage

⅓ cup sliced cherry tomatoes

⅓ cup julienne-cut sweet pepper

⅓ cup bias-cut burdock root

⅓ cup daikon radish, cut into half moons

⅓ cup chopped almonds, soaked and rinsed (see page 153) (optional)

When has the unknown been your teacher?

In your blender purée all of the ingredients for the soup base. Pour the puréed soup base through a milk bag or cheesecloth to remove the lemongrass and ginger pulp.

Next pour a small amount of the soup base over the kale and squeeze/massage it. This will soften the kale and make it more palatable. Divide the softened kale and all other veggies into your soup bowls and top off with the soup base.

I Am Authentic

KOI TEOW, MISO-BASED SOUP
(HOT, SWEET, SPICY, AND SALTY THAI SOUP)

Serves 1 as a main course or 2–3 as a soup course

VEGGIES

½ cup spiralized daikon noodles (see page 23)

½ cup chopped veggies (use two or more of the
   following: shiitake mushrooms, sunchokes, purple
   cabbage, carrot, burdock, zucchini, or fennel)

2 tablespoons chopped cilantro

FOR THE BROTH

1½ cups hot water

1 tablespoon red miso

1 tablespoon agave nectar

1 tablespoon lime juice

scant ⅛ teaspoon smashed garlic

Prepare all veggies and heat a kettle of water.

Place miso into a bowl and add a little hot water to dissolve the miso.
Add lime juice, agave nectar, and garlic. Then add the rest of your hot
water. Stir well and add all the veggies. Taste and adjust the sweet,
sour, salty flavors and chile, if needed. Add a few drops of toasted
sesame chili oil. This soup is bold and tasty.

*Daikon, a sweet white radish, aids in fat and protein
digestion and helps the body assimilate oils.*

What do you really
have faith in?

I Am Dazzling

CAESAR SALAD

Serves 4

1 small romaine lettuce head
½ cup capers
3 slices **I Am Fun** Almond Toast (see page 59)
1 cup Peppery Avocado Dressing (see page 33)

Wash and drain romaine leaves. Slice into bite-size pieces and place in salad bowl. Cut almond toast into small square croutons.

Toss lettuce with capers, croutons and dressing. Divide into 4 servings and sprinkle with **I Am Focused** Brazil Nut Parmesan Cheese (see page 56).

What is your biggest
surprise in life?

PEPPERY AVOCADO CAESAR DRESSING

Makes 2 cups salad dressing

1 cup avocado
2 tablespoons lemon juice
1 tablespoon olive oil
1 cup + 2 tablespoons fresh water
1 teaspoon salt
1 teaspoon freshly ground black pepper
Pinch of cayenne pepper

Blend all ingredients in your blender until smooth, creamy, and dazzling!

I Am Giving

MARINATED KALE SALAD

Serves 4

1 cup marinated shiitake mushrooms
  (see page 155)
4 cups shredded kale
¼ cup hijiki seaweed (presoak for 2 hours, drain)
1 cup shredded carrots
1 cup julienne-cut cucumbers
½ cup sesame seeds to garnish

FOR THE MARINADE
½ cup olive oil
⅓ cup fresh orange juice
2½ tablespoons Nama Shoyu (see page 153)
2½ tablespoons rice vinegar
½ tablespoon sesame oil
½ jalapeño pepper
¼ teaspoon salt

What are you
afraid to give?

Blend all ingredients until well combined.

Slice shiitake mushrooms into thin strips and marinate in ¼ cup lemon juice and ¼ cup Nama Shoyu. Set aside.

In large bowl place kale, drained hijiki, carrots, and cucumbers. Drizzle with marinade and toss until well coated. Remove shiitake mushrooms from liquid and add them to salad mixture. Toss lightly. Divide salad onto four plates and garnish with sesame seeds.

I Am Purified

BURDOCK SALAD

Makes ½ cup

FOR THE SAUCE
2 large dates
2 tablespoons chopped tomato
¼ teaspoon chopped garlic
¼ teaspoon chopped ginger
¼ teaspoon chopped jalapeño
1 tablespoon chopped scallion
¼ cup lemon juice
¼ cup + 1 tablespoon Nama Shoyu (see page 153)
½ teaspoon sesame oil
Pinch of white pepper

VEGGIES
1½ cups julienne-cut burdock
½ cup julienne-cut carrot
¼ cup julienne-cut purple cabbage (optional)

When is less
more?

I think it's best to make the sauce for this recipe first, before you julienne cut your veggies. Then you can dress the veggies as soon as they are cut. (Burdock will oxidize very rapidly!)

It's easiest to make this sauce in a mortar with pestle. If you have one, start by adding all but the liquid ingredients and mash until you have a smooth paste. Incorporate the liquid ingredients next.

If you'll be using a food processor, use the smallest one you may have. And again start with just the non-liquid ingredients. Begin to process. You will need to scrape down the sides frequently until all ingredients are chopped super-fine. Add the liquids and process again.

Julienne the veggies and toss them in the marinade. If you have a dehydrator, place the marinated salad in a metal bowl and dehydrate for 30 minutes at 115°. This will soften the burdock, and the marinade will penetrate the veggies nicely.

Burdock root is a powerful antioxidant, which protects against cancer by preventing cell mutation.

I Am Sprightly

MARINATED DAIKON SALAD

Makes 1½ cups

FOR THE MARINADE
¼ teaspoon very finely chopped jalapeño
¼ teaspoon very finely chopped garlic
¼ teaspoon very finely chopped ginger
¼ cup fresh water
¼ cup Nama Shoyu
2 tablespoons apple cider vinegar
2 teaspoons agave nectar
3 drops toasted sesame oil

FOR THE VEGGIES
1½ cups julienne-cut daikon
¼ cup finely diced red sweet pepper
1 scallion finely sliced on the bias
1 large date, chopped

FOR THE GARNISH
Black sesame seeds
2 tablespoons shredded purple cabbage

Place the chopped ingredients for the marinade in a medium bowl and add the liquid ingredients.

Prepare all the veggies and toss into the marinade. Let set for at least 1 hour.

To serve, you can either leave the veggies in the marinade or drain. Either way a small rice bowl may be best. Sprinkle with the cabbage and black sesame.

I Am Fabulous

THAI GREEN PAPAYA SALAD

Serves 3 as a main course or 6 as a salad course

FOR THE DRESSING
2 teaspoons very finely chopped garlic
2 teaspoons very finely chopped jalapeño
¼ cup lime juice
1 tablespoon agave nectar
2 teaspoons red miso paste

Where could you lighten up?

FOR THE SALAD BASE
4 cups grated green papaya
1 cup grated carrot
¾ cup sliced cherry tomatoes
40 Thai basil leaves, rough-chopped

GARNISH
⅔ cup chopped **I Am Spirit** Teriyaki Almonds
   (see page 37)

If you have a mortar and pestle you can make this sauce in it and avoid the fine chopping. Begin by pounding the garlic and chile into a paste, being careful of flying chile juice and your eyes! After you have reduced the chile and garlic to a paste, add all other dressing ingredients. Next prepare the salad base and massage in the dressing. Divide onto plates and top with chopped **I Am Spirit** Teriyaki Almonds.

I Am Alive

HOMEMADE SAUERKRAUT AND KIM CHEE

Makes about 16 cups Sauerkraut

2 heads green or purple cabbage, or a mixture (purple cabbage will turn your kraut pink)
2 tablespoons salt
2 tablespoons caraway seeds (optional)

or . . .

Makes about 16 cups Kim Chee*

2 large heads cabbage: Napa, green, or purple, or a mixture (purple cabbage will turn your Kim Chee pink)
2 large carrots
¾ pound daikon radish
½ pound burdock root
1 red sweet bell pepper
2 tablespoons salt
½ cup minced ginger
3 tablespoons minced garlic
3 minced jalapeños
1 bunch scallions, sliced on the bias
1 ounce hijiki (optional)

——— ❧ ———

What do your friends
love about you?

---

* Kim chee is very flexible. I like to cut all my veggies a little differently so in the end they are distinguishable. For instance, the carrots could be cut into half moons, burdock sliced on the bias, sweet pepper julienned, and the daikon full moons. The variations on kim chee and sauerkraut are endless, and the boundaries can overlap. You can add apples and onions to kraut, and fruits such as pineapple, firm peaches, and other stone fruits, flowering vegetable tops, radishes, or wild greens that grow in your area to kim chee.

Note: This makes a medium-spicy kim chee.

Making kraut is a fun and amazing process. Invite over a few friends to help you and it will be an absolute breeze.

You can purchase special crocks (see Resource Guide page 163) to make sauerkraut and kim chee, or you can start out using food-grade plastic buckets. If your local co-op or health food store has a bulk miso and/or nut butter department, chances are they'll let you have their old buckets. If not, you can use an old crockpot liner (they just aren't very big). For this recipe I use a three-gallon plastic bucket.

A few other things to have ready: a ceramic or glass plate that will fit about two-thirds down into the bucket and sit horizontally on top of your cabbage. The plate will act as part of a press; the other half will be a large mason jar full of water. (I use an eight-cup jar.) You will also need your largest mixing bowl. All these items should be sterilized with very hot water. Lastly a fresh bath towel as well as a clean dish towel will be needed.

Whew! So now that your equipment is ready to go, you can make some kraut/kim chee.

Cut the bottom of the core off and remove the first few outer leaves of the cabbage. Shred all of the cabbage (you can do this by hand, with a mandolin slicer, or food processor with the slicing blade). Chop all other veggies as well if you are making kim chee. Place into the large mixing bowl and toss with the salt and other ingredients. If your bowl isn't so big, do it in batches.

Now that all your cabbage is cut, salted, and spiced, pack it into your fermentation vessel. Place the vessel on the floor or on a chair to get some good leverage. Use your fist, a kitchen mallet, or the pestle from a large mortar and pestle to help you pack the cabbage in tight. Wipe down the sides so there is no cabbage stuck to the inside of the bucket. This will greatly help in keeping unwanted molds and bacteria out of the mix. Place the plate on the packed cabbage; wiggle it around some to make sure there are no air bubbles trapped under the plate, and top with the weight (your jar of water). Then wrap the bucket and the jar

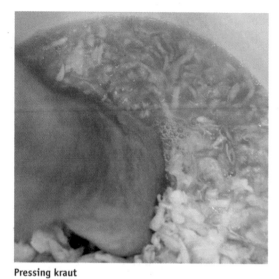

Pressing kraut

Placing plate on kraut

Weighting plate down

Wrapping fermentation vessel with towel

with a towel so no critters can get in; set aside for nature to work her magic. If after packing, the water level from the cabbage hasn't risen above the plate, don't worry—it should within a few hours. Just check later and make sure it has; if it is still below the plate, boil and let cool some water. When cool, pour enough to just cover the plate. Store wherever you like, just remember to check on your baby's progress daily. If mold should appear, do not worry. Simply scrape it away and remove any moldy cabbage. Tightly repack the cabbage and wipe down the sides of your vessel. Wash your plate and weight and place them on the kraut again and wrap with a clean towel. Only the parts exposed to air will mold. That is why it's important that the water level stay above your plate.

The kraut/kim chee will be finished in about three to seven days. Your own preference as to how sour, soft, or crunchy you like your kraut/kim chee will be your guide. It will get stronger and softer daily. Temperature will affect the time needed to complete the ferment; heat will speed up the process, and cold will slow it down. So taste your kraut daily. Your taste buds will let you know when it's done. When the kraut/kim chee has achieved the taste and texture you desire, pack into storage containers and place in the fridge. This will all but stop the fermentation process.

If you plan on making another batch, save a small amount of the kraut and a cup of the liquid as a seed starter for your next batch. Mix in the seed before you pack the next batch into your fermentation vessel.

In whose presence
are you most alive?

I Am Nourished

WAKAME SALAD

Makes 2 cups

1 ounce wakame (presoak for 1 hour in fresh water)
2 tablespoons Nama Shoyu (see page 153)
2 tablespoons agave nectar
1 tablespoon lemon juice
1 teaspoon toasted sesame oil
1 teaspoon finely chopped garlic
1 teaspoon finely chopped ginger
1 teaspoon finely chopped jalapeño
Pinch of white pepper

Drain wakame and julienne it as fine as possible. Assemble all other ingredients and toss together with wakame. Let the seaweed marinate for at least 1 hour.

Sea vegetables contain ten to twenty times the minerals as land plants. These minerals include calcium, iron, potassium, iodine, magnesium, and essential trace minerals.

They are also a great source of vitamins D, E, K and B-complex.

— ❀ —

How do you nourish
yourself?

I Am Creative:
Dressings, Sauces, and Toppings

—— ❀ ——

"Thoughts of lack manifest as
limitation. Thoughts of abundance
manifest as success and happiness.
Failure and success are but two ends
of the same stick."

—Ernest Holmes

I Am Content

FABULOUS FIG BALSAMIC DRESSING

Makes 2 cups

10 soaked Black Mission figs (presoak in 1 cup water for
  2 hours, reserve water)
⅓ cup balsamic vinegar
1 cup olive oil
½ teaspoon jalapeño pepper, finely chopped, with seeds
1 teaspoon salt
1 teaspoon lemon juice
¼ teaspoon black pepper

Blend all ingredients until smooth, starting slow and adding reserved
fig water if necessary. This dressing is thick and creamy.

——— ❀ ———

Are you fulfilled?

I Am Gentle

COCONUT LIME DRESSING

Makes about 3 cups

2 cups coconut milk (see page 91)
⅔ cup lime juice
¼ cup agave nectar
¾ teaspoon salt
1 jalapeño pepper
¼ cup coconut oil
1 teaspoon lecithin powder

Blend all ingredients until smooth and creamy. Gently toss your favorite greens in this light and tangy dressing.

Are you
a gold medalist
in receiving?

I Am Intentional

CITRUS GARLIC DRESSING

Makes 1½ cups

1 cup olive oil
¼ cup lemon juice
¼ cup orange juice
2 teaspoons chopped garlic
1 teaspoon salt
Zest of ⅓ orange*

Is your life aligned
with your highest
intentions?

---

* Be sure to only use the zest (the colored part of the rind).
Otherwise you will impart a bitter taste to your dressing. You may
also want to add a little agave nectar or sweetener to this dressing
if you like it on the sweeter side.

Place all ingredients in the carafe of your blender. Blend well until all the ingredients are emulsified. Taste the dressing for flavor.

I Am Creamy

HEMP SEED RANCH

Makes 3 cups

¾ cup olive oil
¼ cup lemon juice
2 tablespoons Nama Shoyu (see page 153)
1 cup water
½ cup soaked sunflower seeds (presoak for 2 hours)
1 cup hemp seeds
1 teaspoon garlic
1 tablespoon chopped jalapeño pepper
¾ teaspoon salt
¼ teaspoon black pepper
1 tablespoon dried dill

Blend above ingredients well, starting at low speed and gradually increasing. Then add:

½ cup fresh parsley
½ cup fresh cilantro

Blend again slowly, just until herbs are mixed in and the dressing is speckled green. Store in refrigerator.

How could you be
more of service?

I Am Ravishing

CASHEW RICOTTA/SOUR CREAM

Makes 1½–1¾ cups

1½ cups soaked cashews (see page 153)
½ teaspoon salt
2 tablespoons lemon juice
Approximately ¾ cup fresh water

Are you ever overwhelmed by beauty?

Place the soaked and rinsed cashews in a blender, along with ¼ teaspoon salt, lemon juice, and half the water. Start to blend on low, turning up the speed slowly. Add more water as necessary to keep mixture pulling down to the bottom of the blender. When a semi-smooth "ricotta" consistency has been achieved, taste your creation. You may need to add a little more salt or lemon juice; this is also how to turn this recipe into sour cream. This will depend on how diluted the cashews become, as different blenders require more or less water to achieve the right consistency.

Now your ricotta is ready for use in many of our other recipes. This will store nicely in a squirt bottle. (An empty honey bottle or something similar will work fine and make for cute presentation.)

Note: You can change the flavor or color of this cheese very easily by adding one or more of the following: cumin powder, turmeric powder, parsley, cilantro, or bell pepper. Be imaginative and let your creative juices flow! (Just remember, if you're going to be using cilantro, parsley, or bell pepper, chop them first and add them from the beginning so they have a chance to be well incorporated.)

I Am Cheery

CATSUP

Makes about 2 cups

2 dozen sun-dried tomato halves, and
½ dried chipotle chile, soaked in 3 cups of fresh water
    for 2 hours. Reserve 1 cup of soak water.
½ teaspoon finely chopped garlic
¾ teaspoon salt
1 tablespoon agave nectar

Drain the tomato and chile. Place all the ingredients into your blender.
Blend until smooth. Use the extra soak water only if necessary.

I Am Spicy

JALAPEÑO MINT CHUTNEY

What have you
overcome?

Makes 1½ cups

5 soaked Black Mission figs (presoak in 1½ cups of fresh
    water for 2 hours)
2 tablespoons raw coconut oil
1 tablespoon chopped jalapeño pepper, with seeds
½ teaspoon salt
¼ cup loosely packed spearmint leaves
¾ cup coconut milk (see page 91)

Drain figs and reserve ¼ cup of the soaking liquid. Add figs, soaking
liquid, and all remaining ingredients to your blender. Purée until smooth
and creamy and all the coconut oil has been emulsified.

This sauce is sweet and spicy.

I Am Awesome

SALSA VERDE

Makes 3 cups

2 cups avocado
½ chopped jalapeño
¼ cup packed chopped cilantro
6 tablespoons lime juice
4 chopped green onions
½ teaspoon chopped garlic
1 teaspoon salt
½ teaspoon cumin
⅛ teaspoon freshly ground black pepper
¼ teaspoon dried Mexican oregano
¼ cup or so fresh water

What ingredient would you add to your life?

Place all ingredients into a blender. Blend on high until all ingredients make a smooth salsa. You may need to add more water.

At the restaurant we keep this salsa in a squirt bottle, but if you prefer a chunky salsa you can smash and mix the ingredients together with a fork. Just make sure you've chopped your garlic, green onion, and cilantro very fine. Also, you'll omit the water and use a little less lime juice.

For an authentic salsa verde, add fresh tomatillos when in season and adjust spice.

Where has your desire for comfort and security cost you your aliveness?

I Am Impeccable

SMOKY MOLÉ

Makes 2 cups

Presoak for 4 hours, reserve liquid:
2 dozen sun-dried tomato halves, soaked in 2 cups water
2 chipotle chiles, soaked in ¼ cup water

1 tablespoon lime juice
1½ teaspoons salt
1 large avocado
1½ teaspoons cumin powder
3 tablespoons raw cacao powder
¼ cup olive oil
3 large dates
1 cup of soak water from tomatoes and chile (or fresh
   water)

Drain your tomatoes and chile, reserving the water from each sepa-
rately. Place the tomatoes, chipotle chile, and all other ingredients into
a blender. Taste the reserved tomato water. If it's bitter or you prefer,
use fresh water, but be sure to use the chipotle water if you like it spicy.
Add 1 cup of liquid to the blender and start by pulsing. Increase speed
gradually, scraping down sides as necessary. You may need to add a little more liquid. You'll want enough liquid so the blender is able to pull
the ingredients from the top down through the bottom. Stop blending
when a smooth texture is achieved.

This sauce is smoky, spicy, and one of our favorites.

What can people
count on you for?

I Am Receptive

SUN-DRIED TOMATO MARINARA SAUCE

Makes 2 cups

2 dozen sun-dried tomato halves (presoak in 2 cups water for 4 hours, reserve water)

⅓ cup olive oil

1 teaspoon chopped garlic

35 chopped basil leaves

¼ teaspoon (heaping) freshly ground black pepper

½ teaspoon salt

½ jalapeño pepper

2 teaspoons lemon juice

1 teaspoon agave nectar or other sweetener

1 cup soak water or fresh water

Drain the tomato halves and reserve the liquid. Place the tomato halves and all other ingredients into your blender (excluding the water). Taste the reserved tomato water; if it's not bitter use that in lieu of the fresh water and add it to the blender as well. Start by pulsing. Increase speed gradually, scraping down sides as necessary. You may need to add a little more liquid. You'll want enough liquid so the blender is able to pull the ingredients from the top down through the bottom. Stop blending when a smooth texture is achieved.

What do you love
about your mother?

—❀—

In what area
of your life
could you bring
more light?

I Am Light

TZATZIKI

Makes 1¾ cups

2 cups soaked cashews (see page 153)
¼ cup + 1 tablespoon lemon juice
¾ teaspoon salt
½ cup fresh water
1 bunch mint
1 teaspoon agave nectar

Rinse and drain the cashews. Place all ingredients in your blender. Purée until smooth.

I Am Attentive

SPICY TAHINI SAUCE

Makes almost 2 cups

¾ cup coconut milk (see page 91)
¼ cup white miso
1 jalapeño pepper
¼ cup almond butter
½ teaspoon cayenne pepper
1½ tablespoons minced garlic
½ cup raw tahini
3 tablespoons lemon juice

Blend all ingredients until creamy. This sauce is great on salad greens or steamed grains.

In what way
has the universe
dealt you
a royal flush?

I Am Graceful

ALMOND OR HEMP SEED PESTO

Makes 1½–2 cups

1 tablespoon chopped garlic
¾ teaspoon salt
3 bunches basil (leaves only)
¾ cup olive oil
1 tablespoon lemon juice
¼ cup raw almond butter
or
1 cup hemp seeds

Can you give up
blame?

Place all ingredients except for the almond butter or hemp seeds in the bowl of a food processor fitted with the "S" blade. Pulse and scrape down sides of bowl until all the ingredients have reached a pretty smooth texture. While running, add the almond butter or hemp seeds. (Some people like their pesto chunky. Use your own judgment as to when to add the butter or seeds.)

Your pesto is now ready to use. This stores well in an airtight container in the refrigerator.

I Am Focused

BRAZIL NUT PARMESAN CHEESE

Makes 1½ cups

1 cup Brazil nuts
1 teaspoon chopped garlic
⅓ teaspoon salt

In the bowl of a food processor fitted with the "S" blade, process until fluffy. At Café Gratitude this is one of our most popular garnishes.

*Brazil nuts are high in selenium, an essential trace
mineral that acts as a potent antioxidant, which assists
in turning the waste product hydrogen peroxide into water
in the body.*

— ❀ —

If you look at how
you spend your time,
what would you say
the focus of your life is?

I Am Peaceful:
Bread, Crackers, and Tortillas

When Matthew and I first shifted our diet to eating mostly live foods, we thought we were really going to miss our favorite bakeries and breads. I started making sprouted grain rolls to help us transition and then one day noticed that we weren't craving them anymore. Since then I have created live versions of some of our bakery favorites.

———— ❀ ————

"The first step
to bringing peace
into the world
is to realize the peace
that already dwells
within you."

-Anonymous

I Am Fun

ALMOND TOAST

Makes about 15 slices

½ cup soaked almonds (see page 153)
2 cups almond nut milk pulp (see page 93)
⅓ cup flax meal
1 cup veggie pulp
1 teaspoon garlic
1 teaspoon salt
½–1 cup carrot juice

Rinse and drain your almonds. Chop coarsely, and mix well with all ingredients except the carrot juice.

Now add ½ cup of the carrot juice and mix well. Your dough should resemble the consistency of bread dough. You'll want it dry enough to shape into a log (not soupy or runny at all) but wet enough to stick together.

Have ready one, possibly two, dehydrator trays topped with the grid sheet.

Now that your dough is ready, shape it into a log. At the restaurant we make a log about 3 inches wide and 2 inches high. It's probably best to make the log on top of a cutting board. Just turn out the dough onto your cutting board and begin to shape using the palms of your hands until you have a log in the shape you desire. Now make slices in the log about a half-inch wide. Place the slices onto the trays topped with the grid sheet.

Dehydrate at 145° for 1 hour, and then turn down the temperature to 115° until crisp and no moisture remains.

You can easily add your favorite herbs and spices to this recipe. Some of my favorites are:

Herbs de Provence Almond Toast

Rosemary Garlic: 1 tablespoon finely chopped garlic, ¼ cup olive oil, 3 tablespoons dried rosemary

Herbs de Provence: 2 tablespoons Herbs de Provence, ¼ cup olive oil

Pumpernickel Rye: 1 tablespoon caraway seed, ¾ cup raw carob powder, 2 tablespoons agave nectar

Curry Dill: 4 tablespoons curry powder, 2 tablespoons dill, 8 soaked figs (chopped fine), ½ teaspoon salt

Sun-Dried Tomato Basil: 12 sun-dried tomato halves (soak for 4 hours in enough water to cover generously; drain before using), 20 large basil leaves (chiffonade the basil as well as the tomato halves), ¼ cup olive oil

When did you last
skip down the street?

I Am Original

ONION BREAD

1¼ pounds sweet onions, peeled
½ cup ground sunflower seeds
½ cup ground golden flax seeds
¼ cup olive oil
1½ ounces Nama Shoyu (see page 153)
3 tablespoons agave nectar

Put onions in food processor with "S" blade and process until small pieces, but not mush. Put into mixing bowl with other ingredients and mix thoroughly. The flax will absorb the liquid. With moistened fingers, smooth dough onto grid dehydrator sheets lined with a Teflex sheet. Spread to about ¼ inch thick. Dehydrate at 145° for 1 hour, and then reduce temperature to 115° and dehydrate until dry. Break into pieces or cut with pizza cutter and store in airtight container.

What is true
about you?

I Am Relishing

PIZZA CRUST/BUCKWHEAT CRACKERS

Makes about 40 pieces

Presoak for 8 hours, rinse, and drain:
2 cups whole-grain buckwheat*
2⅔ cups sunflower seeds

1 tablespoon chopped garlic
2 cups veggie pulp (left from making juice)
2 teaspoons salt
1 tablespoon + 2 teaspoons Italian herbs
¼ cup ground flax seeds
½ cup + 2 tablespoons olive oil
1½ cups carrot juice

We always say,
if you aren't
relishing
something
then release it!

---

* Be sure to rinse the buckwheat very well, as this will make for a
  much more pleasant cracker.

In the bowl of a food processor fitted with the "S" blade,* purée the
rinsed and drained seeds and grain, along with the rest of the ingredients. Scrape down the sides of the bowl often until you achieve a creamy
texture.

Prepare five dehydrator trays with both the grid and Teflex sheets. Next,
moisten hands with carrot juice or water. Place one-fifth of the mixture on top of the Teflex sheet. Moisten hands again and begin to spread
the mixture out into a layer about ¼ inch thick, making sure there are
no holes and the mixture is evenly spread. This should fit onto five
sheets. With a butter knife, score each sheet into four squares. Then
score again to make the squares into rectangles, the shape we use in
the restaurant. Feel free to use your imagination and shape or score
into any other configuration you desire. Dehydrate at 145° for 1 hour

and then reduce the temperature to 115°. When the tops of the crackers are dry to the touch, you can flip them out onto the grid sheet and peel away the Teflex sheet—this will allow them to dry faster.

Feel free to add your favorite herbs and spices.

The crackers will store at least one week in an airtight container.

---

* If you happen to have a Kitchen Aid mixer with the meat grinder attachment, you might want to use it for this recipe. Just process all ingredients (minus the liquids) through it instead of the food processor. Then add all of the olive oil, and enough carrot juice as necessary to create a sticky batter.

I Am Releasing

FLAX CRACKERS

Makes about 24 crackers

Presoak at least 8 hours:
2½ cups flax seeds (see page 153)

1 cup carrot juice
1 cup carrot pulp
½ teaspoon freshly ground black pepper
1 teaspoon salt

Combine all ingredients in a bowl. Mix thoroughly with hands or use a Kitchen Aid, especially if you are doing a double or triple batch.

Prepare three dehydrator trays with both the grid and Teflex sheets. Next, moisten hands with carrot juice or water. Now place one third of the mixture on top of the Teflex sheet. Moisten hands again and begin to spread the mixture out into a layer about ¼ inch thick, making sure there are no holes and the mixture is evenly spread. This should fit onto three sheets. With a butter knife, score into four squares. Then score again to make the squares into rectangles, the shape we use in the restaurant. Feel free to use your imagination and shape or score into any other configuration you desire. Dehydrate at 115°. When the tops of the crackers are dry to the touch, you can flip them out onto the grid sheet and peel away the Teflex sheet—this will allow them to dry faster.

You can also add your favorite herbs and spices. My favorite addition is smoked salt and shallot.

The crackers will store at least one week in an airtight container.

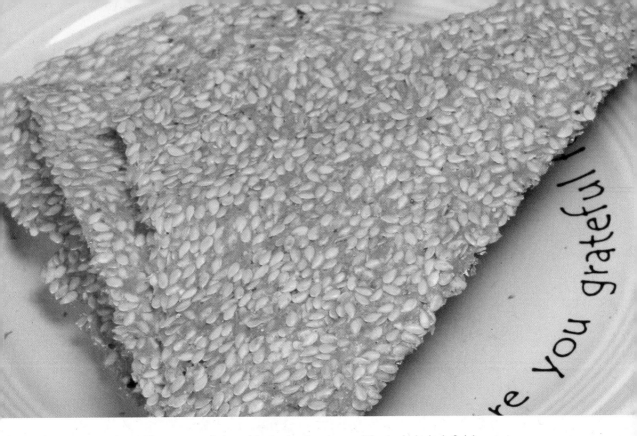

Flax, one of the oldest plants ever cultivated, is helpful in prevention of disease and infection. Flax seed oil is the highest known source of essential omega-3 fatty acids. Flax seeds are also the richest known source of lignans and phytoestrogens, both known anti-carcinogens.

What could you release
(let go of) today, making
room for something new
to come into your life?

I Am Bueno

SPINACH TORTILLAS (see photo page 57)

Makes 4 tortillas

8 ounces fresh spinach (washed and dried)
⅛ teaspoon salt
1 tablespoon flax meal
1 tablespoon lemon juice

For whom or what can you kneel and kiss the ground?

In the bowl of your food processor fitted with the "S" blade, purée the spinach into a paste. Scrape down the bowl of the processor if necessary. Add remaining ingredients and purée again.

Have ready one dehydrator tray fitted with both a grid and a Teflex sheet. Place all of your tortilla dough onto the Teflex sheet. Dip hands into fresh water and begin to smooth out the dough. You're looking to make a thin layer that will cover most of the square Teflex sheet. After you have achieved this, score a plus symbol with a butter knife to create four squares. Dehydrate at 145° for 1 hour and then turn down the temperature to 115° until tortillas are dry but still pliable. Flip the sheet of tortillas over and dry the other side for just a short while. It's easy to dehydrate your tortillas too long because they are so thin. If this happens, don't worry—you can save them! Either a spray bottle with fresh water or your moistened fingertips will do the trick to moisten them just enough to be pliable again.

At the Café, we make our tortillas square, but feel free to make them any shape you like. At home I like to make my tortillas round. This recipe will also work great with arugula or mustard greens. Keep in mind that they are spicier than spinach, so maybe only use half spicy greens mixed with spinach. Fresh corn in season and carrot tortillas also are delicious. Don't forget that you can add herbs and spices like fresh oregano, cilantro, cumin seeds, or chili powder.

I Am Generous:
Entrees

Every day, people are surprised when they see the variety of dishes available at Café Gratitude. I think they expect to see wonderful salads, blended soups, and perhaps pâtés, but not enchiladas, or falafels, or deep-dish pizza! I think we have been conditioned to think that we have to suffer or sacrifice to eat healthy, nutritious meals. Perhaps that's one of the thoughts that continue to threaten our health. Consider that you can experience all the flavors, all the textures, all the pleasures that you associate with your favorite foods, and eat food that is not only good for you but heals you as well.

Food is medicine and medicine is food.

Entrees simply require a bit more preparation and planning ahead. They can easily be assembled at the time of serving, ending the often hectic rush of getting food out of the oven, onto a plate, and served while still hot. Many of our pâtés and fillings can be used in a variety of recipes, thereby simplifying the preparation even more.

Generosity in our practice is simply opening up to the flow; it is the release phase of releasing and receiving. This might look like cleaning out a closet, giving away clothes you no longer wear, or letting go of books you have already read. It might look like inviting someone in for a meal or buying a stranger a cup of tea. It isn't about cause or need; it is simply releasing into the whole of us, keeping things in circulation. In our workshop and logbook we say, "The stuff we store is a block in the flow. If you aren't relishing something, release it!" What could you let go of today? Whom could you share with?

"Unhappiness is the hunger to get,
Happiness is the hunger to give."

–William G. Jordan

I Am Elated

FIVE ENCHILADA FILLINGS

SUN-DRIED TOMATO, CHILE, AND PUMPKIN SEED PÂTÉ

Makes 1½ cups pâté, for 3–6 enchiladas

1 cup soaked pumpkin seeds (see page 153)
8 sun-dried tomato halves (presoak for 4 hours)
½ teaspoon chopped garlic
2 tablespoons lime juice
1 tablespoon Nama Shoyu (see page 153)
1 large chopped date
½ jalapeño pepper, chopped
2 bias-cut scallions
3–6 **I Am Bueno** Spinach Tortillas (see page 66)

Rinse and drain seeds and tomatoes.

Place all ingredients minus the scallions into the bowl of a food processor fitted with the "S" blade. Purée into a semi-smooth pâté.

Place pâté into a bowl and fold in the scallions.

Place ¼–½ cup of the pâté down the middle of a tortilla and roll up. Spoon the following over top of the enchilada before serving: **I Am Ravishing** Cashew Sour Cream (see page 48), and **I Am Awesome** Salsa Verde (see page 50).

GREEN CHILE, LIME, AND CILANTRO SUN SEED PÂTÉ

Makes 1½ cups pâté, for 3–6 enchiladas

1 cup soaked sunflower seeds (presoak for 4 hours, see page 153)

1 jalapeño pepper

¾ teaspoon chopped garlic

3 tablespoons lime juice

1 chopped scallion

½ cup packed, chopped cilantro

½ teaspoon salt

3–6 **I Am Bueno** Spinach Tortillas (see page 66)

Rinse and drain seeds.

Place all ingredients into the bowl of a food processor fitted with the "S" blade. Purée into a smooth pâté.

Place ¼–½ cup of the pâté down the middle of a tortilla and roll up. Spoon the following over top of the enchilada before serving: **I Am Ravishing** Cashew Sour Cream (see page 48), and **I Am Awesome** Salsa Verde (see page 50).

RED PEPPER CASHEW CHEESE PÂTÉ

Makes about 2¼ cups pâté, for 4–8 enchiladas

1¼ cups soaked cashews (see page 153)
1 cup diced red bell pepper
2½ tablespoons lime juice
¼ teaspoon chopped garlic
¾ teaspoon salt

Place all ingredients into the bowl of a food processor fitted with the "S" blade. Purée into a smooth pâté.

Place ¼–½ cup of the pâté down the middle of a tortilla and roll up. Spoon the following over top of the enchilada before serving: **I Am Awesome** Salsa Verde (see page 50).

> **Note:** If you have leftovers of this wonderful pâté, you can dehydrate it to make wonderful cheesy crackers.

MANGO SUN SEED PÂTÉ

Makes 1½ cups pâté, for 3–5 enchiladas

1 cup soaked sunflower seeds (see page 153)
½ finely chopped jalapeño
½ teaspoon chopped garlic
1 tablespoon red miso
2 tablespoons lime juice
½ teaspoon salt
1 thinly sliced bias-cut scallion
¾ cup chopped fresh ripe mango

Rinse and drain the sunflower seeds. Set up your food processor with the "S" blade. Purée the sunflower seeds along with the jalapeño, garlic, miso, salt, and lime juice. Turn out into a bowl when you have achieved a smooth consistency. Fold in the scallion and mango.

Roll up on **I Am Bueno** Spinach Tortilla (see page 66), and spoon **I Am Ravishing** Cashew Sour Cream (see page 48) and **I Am Awesome** Salsa Verde (see page 50) before serving.

MIXED FRUIT FILLING

Makes 3–6 enchiladas

1¾ cups chopped fruit
(use three or more of the following: papaya, pineapple, apple, cherry, tomato, tangerine, orange, strawberry, blueberry, or red pepper)
¼ cup coconut flakes
¼ teaspoon finely chopped garlic
½ teaspoon finely chopped jalapeño
¼ teaspoon finely chopped ginger
¼ teaspoon salt
1 tablespoon chopped cilantro

Dice your chosen fruit in quarter-inch pieces. Now mix all ingredients together, including the coconut and salt.

Roll up on **I Am Bueno** Spinach Tortilla, and top with **I Am Ravishing** Cashew Sour Cream (see page 48) and **I Am Awesome** Salsa Verde (see page 50) before serving.

When do you experience
the ecstatic?

I Am Passionate

MARINARA PIZZA

2 pieces **I Am Relishing** Pizza Crust (see page 62)

2 teaspoons **I Am Opulent** Olive Tapenade (see page 16)

2 tablespoons **I Am Receptive** Marinara Sauce (see page 52)

2 tablespoons **I Am Ravishing** Cashew Ricotta (see page 48)

2 teaspoons chiffonade basil

3 tablespoons sliced cherry tomatoes

2 tablespoons micro-greens or sprouts

1 tablespoon **I Am Focused** Brazil Nut Parmesan Cheese (see page 56)

To assemble, top each relishing with half of all above ingredients, in the order listed above. Serve with a side salad.

I Am Sensational

PESTO PIZZA

2 pieces **I Am Relishing** Buckwheat Crust (see page 62)

2 teaspoons **I Am Opulent** Olive Tapenade (see page 16)

2 tablespoons **I Am Graceful** Pesto (see page 55)

2 tablespoons **I Am Ravishing** Cashew Ricotta
  (see page 48)

2 teaspoons chiffonade basil

3 tablespoons sliced cherry tomatoes

2 tablespoons micro-greens or sprouts

1 tablespoon **I Am Focused** Brazil Nut Parmesan Cheese
  (see page 56)

To assemble, top each relishing with half of all above ingredients, in the order listed. Serve with a side salad.

What do others say is sensational about you?

I Am Open-Hearted

SMOKY MOLÉ PIZZA

2 pieces **I Am Relishing** Pizza Crust (see page 62)

2 tablespoons **I Am Impeccable** Smoky Molé (see page 51)

2 tablespoons **I Am Ravishing** Cashew Ricotta (see page 48)

3 tablespoons cubed avocado

2 teaspoons chopped cilantro

3 tablespoons sliced cherry tomatoes

2 tablespoons micro-greens or sprouts

1 tablespoon **I Am Focused** Brazil Nut Parmesan Cheese
  (see page 56)

To assemble, top each relishing with half of all above ingredients, in the order listed. Serve with a side salad.

With whom have you broken your word?
How about restoring it now?

I Am Mahalo

HAWAIIAN PIZZA

2 pieces **I Am Relishing** Pizza Crust (see page 62)

2 tablespoons **I Am Ravishing** Cashew Ricotta (see page 48)

3 tablespoons cubed avocado

3 tablespoons cubed pineapple

3 tablespoons sliced cherry tomatoes

2 tablespoons micro-greens or sprouts

1 tablespoon **I Am Focused** Brazil Nut Parmesan Cheese
   (see page 56)

To assemble, top each relishing with half of all above ingredients, in
the order listed. Serve with a side salad.

What do you love
about your father?

I Am Vivacious

STUFFED AVOCADO

For each serving you will need the following:

1 ripe medium avocado

¼ cup **I Am Kind** Refried Beans (see page 8)

2 tablespoons **I Am Impeccable** Smoky Molé (see page 51)

2 tablespoons **I Am Ravishing** Cashew Sour Cream (see page 48)

1 tablespoon **I Am Focused** Brazil Nut Parmesan Cheese (see page 56)

Do you have opinions or do your opinions have you?

To assemble, cut avocado in half length-wise. Top each half with two tablespoons of the **I Am Kind** pâté rolled into a ball. Drizzle each half with both the **I Am Impeccable** and **I Am Ravishing.** Sprinkle with **I Am Focused.** Serve with a side salad.

I Am Cheerful

SUN BURGERS

Makes 10 patties

1 cup soaked walnuts (see page 153)
1 cup soaked pumpkin seeds (see page 153)
7 sun-dried tomato halves (presoak in water for 4 hours, reserve liquid)
⅔ cup mushroom stems or tops (any kind will do)
2 tablespoons Nama Shoyu (see page 153)
¼ teaspoon salt
⅓ cup grated carrot
1 teaspoon chili powder
1 teaspoon Italian herbs
½ teaspoon chopped garlic
3 tablespoons olive oil

Rinse and drain seeds and nuts. Drain the tomatoes, reserving the liquid.

Place all the ingredients into a food processor fitted with the "S" blade. Add ½ cup of the soaking liquid and purée. Scrape down and add liquid if necessary to form a paste. Remember, you're looking to create something dry enough to form into patties.

Have ready one dehydrator tray fitted with both a grid and a Teflex sheet. Measure out ¼ cup of your mixture and pat down into a patty and place onto the Teflex sheet. Repeat until you've used all your **I Am Cheerful** mixture. Dehydrate at 145° for 1 hour and then reduce temperature to 115° until about half dry. These will store in the fridge for a few days, no problem.

Pumpkin seeds are extremely high in protein, 28%.

Yo Soy Mucho

MEXICAN GRAIN BOWL

For each serving you will need the following:

½ cup shredded kale

1 cup cooked rice or **I Am Wholehearted** Raw Veggie Rice (see page 24)

⅓ cup **I Am Generous** Guacamole (see page 17)

¼ cup **I Am Fiery** Salsa Fresca (see page 20)

2 tablespoons **I Am Focused** Brazil Nut Parmesan Cheese (see page 56)

¼ cup sprouts

To assemble, simply place the kale in a bowl and arrange all above ingredients on top.

Are you winning the game
of living an inspired life?

Can you see how much you
have already been given?

I Am Accepting

STIR-UNFRY

For each serving you will need the following:

1 cup cooked rice or **I Am Wholehearted** Raw Veggie
   Rice (see page 24)
½ cup **I Am Grateful** Marinated Veggies (see page 18)
1 tablespoon bias-cut scallions
1 tablespoon pine nuts
2 tablespoons marinated sliced shiitakes (see page 155)
Nama Shoyu to taste (see page 153)

GARNISH
1 teaspoon sesame seeds
2 tablespoons **I Am Spirit** Teriyaki Almonds (see page 3)

To assemble, stir together all ingredients; save the garnish. Turn out
onto a plate, and top with sesame and **I Am Spirit** Teriyaki Almonds.
Serve with salad if desired.

Do you adore the
person in the mirror?

I Am Whole

"MACRO" BOWL

For each serving you will need the following:

¾ cup shredded kale

1 cup cooked rice/quinoa or **I Am Wholehearted** Raw
Veggie Rice (see page 24)

⅓ cup **I Am Alive** Kim Chee (see page 38)

¼ cup sprouts

¼ cup grated carrots

GARNISH

2 tablespoons **I Am Spirit** Teriyaki Almonds (see page 3)

To assemble, layer all ingredients in a bowl in the order they appear
above.

—— ❀ ——

Do you invest
more attention
in being grateful
or chasing desires?

I Am Enrolled

NORI ROLLS

Serves 4

4 sheets nori

FOR THE RICE

One recipe **I Am Wholehearted** Raw Veggie Rice, made preferably with daikon radish (see page 24)

FOR THE PÂTÉ

1 cup soaked pumpkin seeds (see page 153)

3 tablespoons scallions

2 tablespoons Nama Shoyu (see page 153)

2 tablespoons chopped ginger

1 teaspoon wasabi powder

FOR THE FILLING

Use any combo of the following: julienne-cut sweet pepper, carrot, cucumber, avocado, marinated mushrooms, kim chee and/or umeboshi plum paste. Feel free to get creative here.

In the bowl of a food processor fitted with the "S" blade, purée all of the pâté ingredients until smooth.

ROLLING

Have ready a small bowl of room-temperature water. Place a sheet of nori on a sushi mat. The sticks of the mat should be horizontal in front of you. (If you don't have one you can use a clean dishtowel.) Spread one-quarter of your pâté evenly on the bottom four-fifths of the sheet of nori. (This will leave the top fifth empty, which should be furthest away from you.) Next gently sprinkle a layer of the "rice" over the pâté. Gently press the rice into the pâté. Now in the middle of the rice and pâté, in a horizontal line lay out your chosen fillings. With a firm yet gentle grip begin to roll the sushi. Using your three middle fingers on both hands to hold the filling in, your thumbs will be doing the rolling while your palms bring some pressure from the top. When the edge of your mat touches the rice, press down slightly on the mat to firm up the roll. Be careful not to roll the mat into your sushi.

Dip a few fingers into the water and wipe them across the exposed nori; the water will act as glue. Now finish rolling. If you're using a mat, wrap the entire roll and gently squeeze the whole roll. Repeat for the remainder of ingredients. Using your sharpest knife, cut the roll into several pieces. (If you're having a hard time cutting the sushi, try wiping the knife between cuts or use a serrated knife.)

Serve with a salad and, if you like, more wasabi, ginger, and Nama Shoyu for dipping.

> *Alginic acid in sea vegetables binds to radioactive and metallic toxins in our bodies, eliminating these harmful substances.*

For whom does
your existence
make a difference?

I Am Creamy

MAC NUT AND NOT CHEESE ALFREDO SAUCE

Serves 2
This is enough sauce for one recipe (serves 2) of
I Am Flowing *Veggie Noodles.*

FOR THE SAUCE
1 cup macadamia nuts (do not soak)
½ cup almond or Brazil nut milk (see page 92)
2 tablespoons chopped scallion
½ teaspoon chopped garlic
¾ teaspoon salt
¼ teaspoon nutmeg
¼ teaspoon white pepper

I Am Flowing Veggie Noodles (see page 23)

Blend all ingredients for sauce until creamy. Taste and adjust seasonings if necessary. Serve with **I Am Flowing** Veggie Noodles and let this luxurious sauce dance over your favorite types and shapes of vegetable noodle.

What would be
possible if you
weren't concerned
about what others
thought?

I Am Festive

CHILES RELLENOS: MACADAMIA-CRUSTED CHEESE-STUFFED GREEN CHILES

Serves 3

3 large mild green chiles, Anaheim or similar variety

FOR THE "CHEESE"
1½ cups soaked cashews (see page 153)
½ teaspoon salt
¾ teaspoon cumin powder
½ teaspoon chopped garlic

FOR THE BATTER
1 cup macadamia nuts
½ cup coconut milk (see page 91)
1 teaspoon chopped jalapeño
½ teaspoon chopped garlic
½ teaspoon salt
½ teaspoon cumin powder

After your cashews have soaked, rinse and drain them. Place cashews and all other "cheese" ingredients into a blender and purée until smooth. Scrape the cheese mixture into a small bowl.

Purée all of the batter ingredients in a blender until smooth. Pour batter into a measuring cup or something deep enough to dip chiles into for coating.

Soak your chiles in hot water for 10 minutes to soften them up. Make a slit in each chile from just under the stem to just above the tip.

Stuff each chile using a spoon with one third of the cheese. Holding onto the stem, dip the chiles into the cup of batter, coating them well. Let drip for just a moment and then place them on a dehydrator tray

with both a Teflex and grid sheet. Dehydrate at 145° for 1 hour, and then turn the temperature down to 115° for 2–3 more hours. Peppers should be slightly soft when done.

Top with **I Am Awesome** Salsa Verde (see page 50).

— ❀ —

What if you
celebrated everything
as part of your
awakening?

I Am Complete

COCONUT CEVICHE

Makes 3–4 cups; serves 3 as a main course, 10 as an appetizer

2 Thai young coconuts (see pages 91 and 155)
1 medium tomato
3 inches of cucumber
⅓ bunch cilantro
1 jalapeño pepper
½ red onion
½ teaspoon garlic
⅓ cup lime juice
1 teaspoon salt
¼ teaspoon freshly ground pepper

Crack open the coconuts and pour off water to drink or reserve for another use. Scrape out coconut meat and julienne into very fine ⅛-inch strips. Cut the strips into 1- to 1½-inch pieces. Place coconut into a 4-cup ceramic or glass bowl.

Wash and dice the tomato and cucumber into ¼-inch pieces. Wash and finely chop the cilantro leaves and stems (use the stems only if not woody). Finely chop the jalapeño, onion, and garlic as well. Mix all remaining ingredients together and marinate for at least 1 hour.

If serving as a main dish, place on top of a small bed of greens and serve with avocado or guacamole, and **I Am Releasing** Flax Crackers (see page 64).

Being complete with someone means
there is nothing in the way of you experiencing love!

I Am Hopeful

PAD THAI

Makes 3 servings as a main course

FOR THE SAUCE
1 cup coconut milk (see page 91)
½ cup raw almond butter
1 teaspoon minced jalapeño
1 tablespoon minced ginger
2 tablespoons Nama Shoyu (see page 153)
1 tablespoon red miso
1 teaspoon minced garlic
2 tablespoons lime juice
2 teaspoons chopped dates
⅛ teaspoon cayenne

"Our entire life . . .
consists ultimately
in accepting ourselves
as we are."

–Jean Anouilh

NOODLE BASE

3 cups spiralized daikon (see "Spiralizer" page 159)

1 cup shredded kale

½ cup julienne-cut red pepper

½ cup grated carrot

1 bias-cut scallion

½ cup cherry tomatoes, cut in half

40 Thai basil leaves

2 tablespoons chopped cilantro

GARNISH

Cucumber slices cut on the bias (3 for each serving)

⅔ cup chopped **I Am Spirit** Teriyaki Almonds
(see page 3)

Whole kale leaf or mesclun mixed greens, for serving
(optional)

To prepare the sauce, place all ingredients into a blender. Blend on high until all the ingredients become creamy and smooth. Taste and adjust flavors if necessary.

Ten minutes or so before serving, dress the noodles. Place all of the prepared ingredients from the noodle base into a large bowl. Toss the noodle base with the sauce we've just made. If you haven't already prepped your garnish, do this while your noodles are marinating.

Fan out and place three of the bias-cut cucumbers on the edge of each plate, and a little mesclun mixed greens or kale leaf off to the other side if using. Place the Pad Thai mixture in the center of each plate, and top with halved tomatoes and chopped **I Am Spirit** Teriyaki Almonds.

—— ❧ ——

What's beyond right
and wrong?

I Am Worthy (of everything wonderful): Beverages

There are so many delicious and nutritious beverages that you can make fresh daily.

Juice is a meal in itself. All fresh-pressed juices are full of nutrients and easy to digest. Adding juice to your diet is a great preventative health measure, and juice fasting therapy is also used to treat medical conditions. When we envisioned Café Gratitude, we saw people sitting at a bar celebrating life with beautiful wine goblets filled with vital nutrient-rich juices, and today that's what you'll see when you walk into any Café Gratitude.

Sometimes customers struggle with the price of a high-quality fresh juice. We have been so conditioned to get super-sized nutrient-poor beverages for a low price. Our response to this concern is, "You are worth it."

Look and see where you stop being worthy of some quality item or experience. Perhaps you can start practicing affirming your worth the next time you get stopped.

We are sharing with you our most popular juice and smoothie recipes; however, you can experiment and create so many wonderful fruit and vegetable juice combinations. Let yourself be creative. Start making and serving fresh juice cocktails in beautiful glasses when celebrating precious moments of life together with those you love.

I Am Aloha

FRESH COCONUT MILK

First crack open the coconut, using a large, sharp cleaver or heavy chef's knife. Hold the coconut flat against a solid surface with the point of the coconut facing up. Keep your fingers well out of the way. With a strong swing, bring down the cleaver or knife about 1½ inches from the top point of the coconut. (Your fingers should be on the other side.)

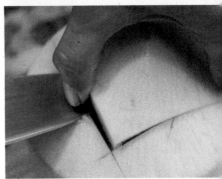

Next, continue around the top three or four more times until you have created a lid you can pry open. Pour the coconut water through a sieve into your blender. Scrape the meat from inside the coconut with a heavy spoon. Be sure to remove small bits of shell from the coconut meat, and if necessary, with a peeler remove any tough brown membranes. Add the cleaned meat to the water and blend on high until smooth. You can enjoy this nutritious milk by itself or in one of our expressions.

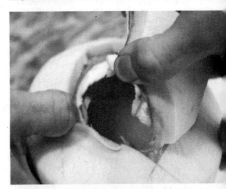

Coconut water, the cloudy but translucent liquid from inside a young coconut, is filtered upward through the tree for nine months, making it a pure, sterile source of hydration. Coconut water is almost chemically identical to blood plasma: in fact, it can be used as a plasma substitute intravenously.

I Am Youthful

LIVE NUT AND SEED MILKS

Makes 6 cups

All our milks at Café Gratitude are made from almonds, Brazil nuts, or hazelnuts. Hemp seeds also make delicious and nutritious milk.

Presoak almonds in fresh water for 12 hours; drain, rinse, and recover with fresh water at least once. You do not need to soak hazelnuts or Brazil nuts, as they do not contain any enzyme inhibitors.

FOR ALMOND MILK
2½ cups soaked almonds

FOR HAZELNUT MILK
2½ cups hazelnuts

FOR BRAZIL NUT MILK
2½ cups Brazil nuts

FOR HEMP SEED MILK
2 cups hemp seeds

Making nut milk is super-easy and very satisfying. If you drink soy milk or another boxed milk product, you'll never go back after making one of these delicious fresh nut or seed milks.

Always rinse and drain your nuts after soaking.

What is a youthful quality
you would like to experience more of?

Now place your chosen nut or seed into the carafe of your blender. Add 6 cups of filtered water and a pinch of salt. Blend on high until the nuts are completely broken down. Be careful not to blend too long, as the friction from the blender will create heat.

Next pour your milk through a nut milk bag and squeeze as much of the moisture out as possible. You now have a delicious fresh nut milk to enjoy on its own, with live granola, or in one of our smoothie recipes.

If you like a sweeter milk, add a little agave or a few dates and/or vanilla. Yum!

> **Note:** Reserve your nut pulp to use in a cake or bread recipe. This will freeze well until you have enough saved to use it.

> *Almonds are the only nuts that are known to alkalize the blood, while all others acid-ify blood. Almonds are also highest of all nuts in arginine, an amino acid that boosts the immune system and inhibits tumor growth.*

How do you nourish yourself?

I Am Nourishing:
Our Favorite Juice Blends

*J*uicing is fun and creative. A Champion or Green Star juicer works well, and for more nutrition and yield we recommend a Norwalk Juice Press—see the back of the book for our resource guide, **I Am Resourceful** (page 163).

Always wash but do not seed or peel your veggies, as you will be wasting much of their nutrition and energy. When juicing a variety of vegetables start with the light-colored ones, juicing the dark orange or red ones last. This way you will be able to pour your juices into a goblet and create some beautiful color combinations. Matthew and I enjoy drinking fresh juice as our sacred time together.

I Am Renewed

FRESH WHEATGRASS JUICE BY THE OUNCE

Fresh wheatgrass juice can be grown and juiced at home. For equipment, see our resource guide, **I Am Resourceful** (page 162). Properly produced wheatgrass juice contains well over a hundred vitamins, minerals, amino acids, enzymes, essential fatty acids, and antioxidants. Wheatgrass juice is highly regarded because it can single-handedly support the human body. It contains an abundance of many nutritious elements, and it is delivered in a natural living state.

I Am Rejuvenated

Do you have enough right now?

SPARKLING WHEATGRASS JUICE COCKTAIL

Makes 16 ounces

6 ounces apple juice
2 ounces lemon juice
½ ounce ginger juice
2 ounces wheatgrass juice

Pour fresh juices into a goblet and then top off with sparkling water.

Next time you are tired,
ask yourself,
"What am I resisting?"

I Am Rich

A SLIGHTLY SWEET GREEN DRINK

Makes 16 ounces

7 ounces cucumber juice
5 ounces apple juice
2 ounces kale juice
2 ounces fennel juice

Pour fresh juices into a goblet and serve.

I Am Worthy

DEEP RED JUICE BLEND

Makes 16 ounces

7 ounces apple juice
5 ounces celery juice
2 ounces kale juice
2 ounces beet juice
Splash of ginger juice

Pour fresh juices into a goblet with a splash of ginger at the end.

—— ❁ ——

What's one thing you have been given in the past 24 hours that has nothing to do with earning it?

—— ❁ ——

Say out loud three times, "I am worthy of everything wonderful!"

I Am Succulent

GRAPEFRUIT JUICE BLEND

Makes 16 ounces

8 ounces grapefruit juice
5 ounces apple juice
3 ounces celery juice
Splash of fennel juice

Pour fresh juices into a goblet, adding a splash of fennel juice at the end and garnishing with a sprig of fresh mint.

What's juicy about your relationships?

I Am Healthy

ALL-GREEN ENERGY DRINK

Makes 16 ounces

8 ounces cucumber juice
5 ounces celery juice
3 ounces kale juice
Splash of lemon juice

Pour fresh juices into a goblet, adding a splash of lemon at the end; garnish with a lemon wedge. We add 1 tablespoon of solé (see page 155) for extra flavor.

Start saying to yourself,
"I am healthy!"
rather than asking yourself,
"Do I look good?"

I Am Charismatic

LIGHTLY SPICED CARROT JUICE

Makes 16 ounces

16 ounces carrot juice
Splash of lime and ginger juice

Pour fresh carrot juice into a goblet, top with a splash of lime and ginger juice, and garnish with a lime wedge.

Under what circumstances are you most present?

I Am Excited

FRESH CUCUMBER JUICE

Makes 16 ounces

16 ounces cucumber juice
1 tablespoon solé (see page 155)

Pour the cucumber juice into a goblet and then add the solé and stir slightly.

I Am Wonderful

WATERMELON JUICE

Be sure to juice the rind and seeds as well! This creates a beautiful pink and green beverage. Pour fresh juice into a goblet and garnish with a sprig of fresh mint.

What do you rebel against?

I Am Sassy

VIRGIN MARGARITA

Makes 16 ounces

2 tablespoons solé (see page 155)
2 tablespoons lemon juice
2 tablespoons agave nectar

*Whose beauty
have you
fallen asleep to?*

Add the above ingredients to your blender and fill to 12 ounces with fresh water, and then fill to 16 ounces with ice. Blend until frosty and serve immediately.

I Am Sassy can be made spectacular by substituting watermelon or cucumber juice for all or part of the water in this recipe.

> *The periodic table contains 94 elements, and Himalayan Crystal Salt contains 84 of these, including every single element of which the human body is composed. Solé, a Himalayan Crystal Salt-water solution, creates pH balance in the body by replenishing electrolytes, improving the body's conductivity, and stimulating circulation.*

*What thrills you
about the times
we live in?*

I Am Bold

SPICY TOMATO JUICE COCKTAIL

Makes 16 ounces

4 ounces carrot juice
4 ounces celery juice
¼ cup chopped tomato
⅓ cup **I Am Fiery** Salsa Fresca (see page 20)
Pinch of cayenne

Blend all of the above ingredients together and pour into a goblet; garnish with a celery stick.

In what way are you
a great lover?

I Am Effervescent

OUR HOUSE GINGERALE

Makes 16 ounces

9 ounces apple juice
7 ounces sparkling water
Splash of ginger juice

Pour fresh juice into a goblet, add sparkling water, and splash with fresh ginger juice to your liking.

Whom do you envy?

I Am Refreshed

OUR HOUSE LEMONADE

Makes 16 ounces

9 ounces apple juice
7 ounces sparkling water
Splash of lemon juice

Pour fresh juice into a goblet, add sparkling water, and splash with fresh lemon juice to your liking. Garnish with a lemon wedge.

— ❀ —

How do you react to
people who are
buoyantly optimistic?

I Am Brand-New:
Our Favorite Smoothies

Making smoothies is another opportunity to be creative, as the possible combinations are endless.

At the Café we offer additions for our smoothies. Here is a list of our offerings—feel free to add them or one of your favorite supplements to any smoothie: Vitamineralgreen, hemp seeds, maca powder, Blue Mana, E3Live, Raw Power, raw cacao, almond butter.

I Am Cool

MINT CHOCOLATE CHIP MILKSHAKE

What do you love about your personality?

Makes 16 ounces

10 ounces **I Am Pleased** Vanilla Hazelnut Ice Cream (see page 145)

5 ounces almond milk (see page 92)

2 heaping tablespoons raw cacao nibs (see page 150)

3 tablespoons chopped dates

10 spearmint leaves

1 teaspoon Vitamineralgreen (see page 156)

½ teaspoon vanilla

A tiny pinch of salt

Blend all ingredients and pour into a frosty glass. The cacao nibs, which are bits of the raw bean, are the chocolate chips!

I Am Luscious

A HEALTHY RAW CHOCOLATE SMOOTHIE

Makes 16 ounces

9 ounces Brazil nut milk (see page 92)
3 soaked Black Mission figs (presoak for 2 hours)
3 tablespoons chopped dates
2 heaping tablespoons raw cacao powder
½ teaspoon vanilla
A tiny pinch of salt

Blend all ingredients together and pour into a frosty glass.

— ❁ —

I Am Lusciously Awake

For what can you acknowledge your community?

MOCHA SMOOTHIE

Makes 16 ounces

7 ounces Brazil nut milk
2 ounces cold-processed espresso
3 soaked Black Mission figs (presoak for 2 hours)
3 tablespoons chopped dates
2 heaping tablespoons raw cacao powder
½ teaspoon vanilla
A tiny pinch of salt

Blend all ingredients together and pour into a frosty glass.

— ❁ —

Do you take quiet time for yourself every day?

I Am Grace

COCONUT ALMOND SMOOTHIE

Makes 16 ounces

8 ounces coconut milk (see page 91)
3 tablespoons + 1 teaspoon chopped dates
3 tablespoons + 1 teaspoon raw almond butter
½ teaspoon vanilla
A tiny pinch of salt

Place all ingredients in your blender and fill to 2 cups with ice. Blend until smooth.

I Am Beautiful

CREAMSICLE MILKSHAKE

Makes 16 ounces

10 ounces **I Am Pleased** Vanilla Hazelnut Ice Cream (see page 145)
8 ounces orange juice
½ teaspoon vanilla
A tiny pinch of salt

Blend all ingredients together and pour into a frosty glass.

— ❀ —

In what way could
you take better care
of yourself?

I Am Delicious

COCONUT MALTED

Makes 16 ounces

8 ounces coconut milk (see page 91)
1 tablespoon almond butter
1 tablespoon maca
¼ cup dates
½ teaspoon vanilla
Pinch of salt

Place all ingredients in blender and add ice to 2-cup level. Blend until smooth and pour into a frosted glass.

I Am Berry Sweet

FRESH STRAWBERRY MILKSHAKE

Makes 16 ounces

8 ounces almond milk (see page 92)
7 medium strawberries
¼ cup dates
½ teaspoon vanilla
A tiny pinch of salt

Place all ingredients in your blender and fill to 2 cups with ice. Blend until smooth.

— ❀ —

For what do you forgive yourself?

— ❀ —

In what way will you take on a younger attitude today?

I Am Anew:
Breakfast

Breakfast is breaking our fast of the night. Starting each day with a glass of warm water with a squeeze of fresh lemon cleanses our system and purifies our blood. Meditating and Pranayama breathing are our favorite way to start a new day. We invite you to create a morning ritual that inspires you!

"Life is a series
of awakenings."

–Sivananda

I Am Bright-Eyed

PECAN PORRIDGE

What do you love about yourself?

Makes about 3 cups or 2 servings

1 large apple
5 large ripe strawberries or other seasonal berries
2½ cups coconut milk (see page 91)
½ cup shelled raw pecans
½ teaspoon vanilla extract
Pinch of salt
Big pinch of cinnamon

Wash, core, and rough-chop the apple. Wash and top the strawberries. Place fruit and all other ingredients into your blender. Pulse to desired consistency, chunky or smooth. Taste and adjust salt, cinnamon, and vanilla if necessary.

Pour into two bowls. Top with a strawberry, a few pecans, and a sprinkle of cinnamon.

I Am Vigorous

MACADAMIA NUT PORRIDGE

Makes about 3 cups or 2 servings

1 large apple
2½ cups coconut milk (see page 91)
½ cup shelled raw macadamia nuts
½ teaspoon vanilla extract
½ teaspoon cinnamon
Pinch of salt

Wash, core, and rough-chop the apple. Place fruit and all other ingredients into your blender. Pulse to desired consistency, chunky or smooth. Taste and adjust salt, cinnamon, and vanilla if necessary.

Pour into two bowls. Top with a macadamia nut and/or sprinkle of cinnamon.

I Am Great

GRANOLA

Makes about 8 cups

1½ cup soaked almonds (see page 153)
½ cup soaked sunflower seeds (see page 153)
½ cup soaked whole buckwheat (see page 153)
7 small apples or 5 cups grated apple
½ cup puréed dates (about 7 large dates)
½ cup cranberries
½ cup dry coconut
½ cup agave nectar
1 teaspoon vanilla
2 teaspoons cinnamon
⅓ teaspoon salt

If you were certain that life is eternal and unfolding perfectly, what would you take on?

Can you bow to all the ways you are and all the ways you are not?

Rinse and drain the grain and seeds. Place into a large bowl.

Grate enough apple to make five cups of grated fruit (about 7 small apples).

In the bowl of a food processor fitted with the "S" blade, purée the dates to a fine paste. If your dates are really dry you can add a little of the apple.

Now, add all of your fruit and the remaining ingredients to your seeds and nuts. Mix well.

Prepare two dehydrator trays with both the grid and Teflex sheets. You can use all of your trays if your dehydrator isn't full of other things, as this will speed up your drying time! Divide your granola mixture into as many parts as trays you will be using. Spread out the granola with your hands and dehydrate at 145° for 1 hour, and then reduce temperature to 115°. When your granola is dry enough to peel off the Teflex sheets, do so and place onto the grid sheets. Continue to dehydrate until dry.

This recipe will easily double or triple. You can also keep it in the fridge for one day if you don't have room to dehydrate all at once.

This recipe is easy to adjust to your liking. If you don't like coconut, leave it out. In other words, be creative! If you use dried fruit, you can add it at the end and it will stay much moister.

I Am Thrilled

CINNAMON ROLLS

Makes 4 rolls

½ cup soaked almonds
2 cups almond nut milk pulp (see page 93)
⅓ cup flax meal
½ cup pitted dates
1½ teaspoons vanilla
1 teaspoon cinnamon
1 teaspoon salt
½–1 cup coconut milk (see page 91)

FOR THE FILLING AND TOPPING
2 cups pecan pieces
½ cup agave nectar
1 teaspoon cinnamon
¼ teaspoon salt
¼ teaspoon vanilla

—— ❀ ——

Who praises you?

Rinse and drain your almonds. Chop coarsely, and mix well with all ingredients except the coconut milk.

Now add ½ cup of the coconut milk, and mix well. Your dough should resemble the consistency of bread dough. Add additional coconut milk if necessary. You'll want it dry enough to roll (not soupy or runny at all) but wet enough to stick together.

Have ready one, possibly two, dehydrator trays topped with the grid sheet.

Now that your dough is ready, roll it out on a Teflex sheet to about ½-inch thickness. Spread the filling evenly on the dough. Reserve some filling for topping. Now roll up like a jelly roll, with moist hands to prevent sticking. Seal the edges of your roll with a little bit of water. Slice the roll into ¾- to 1-inch pieces and place them on a Teflex-lined grid sheet. Now top each roll with a spoonful of topping and dehydrate for 1 hour at 145°. Turn down the temperature to 115° and continue until semi-soft.

These are best served right from the dehydrator, topped with **I Am The Best** Caramel Sauce (see page 147).

I Am Courageous

COLD-PROCESSED COFFEE

Who really knows you?

This method, popular among Dutch settlers in Java in the nineteenth century, steeps coarsely ground coffee in cold, fresh water for up to 24 hours. When filtered, the liquid concentrate or essence may be stored in the refrigerator for up to six weeks or frozen for longer periods. When reconstituted, it becomes a delicious, smooth-tasting, low-acid cup of coffee.

See **I Am Resourceful** (page 162), our resource guide in the back of the book, for information about a Filtron home brewer.

At our cafés we dilute our Fair Trade Organic coffee elixir with steamed nut milks for espresso drinks, and with hot water for Americano-style coffee. Raw chocolate powder added to the steamed milk makes a delicious mocha.

I Am Abundant:
Delicious Desserts and Sweets

Sweets are perhaps the most healing of experiences at Café Gratitude. So many of us have been conditioned to feel guilty about eating sweets and/or we have become addicted to sugar and feel powerless over its influence on our lives and bodies. Sweets were the last foods I could trust myself with as I learned to eat again. Flour, sugar, and butter are the basic ingredients of most desserts and all are difficult to digest, have little nutritional value, and are the source of many diseases associated with inflammation and aging. As much as I loved making desserts that pleased people, I always felt guilty about what I was feeding them.

Today the desserts in the Café are not only beautiful and mouthwateringly delicious, but nutritious as well. We use organic dates, agave nectar, and yacon syrup as sweeteners. None of our desserts contain any refined sugar, flour, or dairy, although it is difficult for people to believe it. Culturally we have come to associate celebrations with unhealthy sweets and foods, but now our organic live desserts offer a new opportunity to truly celebrate life and all its special moments. We have had the privilege of making several wedding cakes, two of which were celebrating our son's and daughter's weddings. It was heartwarming for me to see people not only admire, love, and eat the cakes, but to know also that they were good food.

Abundance is the knowingness of being provided for, always. Just like we know the sun is going to rise. People are often challenged by this notion and ask us, "What about all the people who don't have enough?" Consider that we have no idea what life would look like, how the wealth might be distributed, if we who do have enough were being abundant, were being responsible for all we already have, were interrupting the continual search for more. What do you already have an abundance of that you may be either oblivious to or completely taking for granted?

I Am Rapture

STRAWBERRY SHORTCAKE

Makes one 9-inch cake (you will need a pan with a removable bottom)

FOR THE CAKE
2 cups well packed, finely chopped dates
¾ cup raw unscented coconut butter
¼ cup lemon juice
3 tablespoons vanilla
½ teaspoon salt
2 cups fresh strawberries
9 cups almond flour (see page 162)

FOR THE WHIPPED CREAM
2 cups cashews (see page 153)
2½ cups fresh coconut milk (see page 91)
½ cup agave nectar
2 tablespoons lemon juice
1 tablespoon vanilla
Pinch of salt
2 tablespoons lecithin powder
1 cup raw unscented coconut butter

BETWEEN THE LAYERS
3 cups finely chopped strawberries

GARNISH
Whole or sliced strawberries for decoration

—❀—

*"Wise men count
their blessings—
fools their problems."*

—Anonymous

TO MAKE THE WHIPPED CREAM

Blend all ingredients except the lecithin and coconut butter until smooth. Add lecithin and coconut butter and blend until well incorporated. Pour into a wide, shallow pan and set in fridge for about an hour.

TO MAKE THE CAKE

Place the chopped dates in the bowl of your food processor fitted with the "S" blade. Process until the dates have reached a smooth paste. This may require adding a little water and scraping down the bowl several times. Next, in a standing mixer with the flat paddle or with a hand mixer at low speed, beat the date, coconut butter, lemon juice, vanilla, and salt until smooth. Add flour and mix at a higher speed until well incorporated. When ready, remove from mixer and separate into three equal portions.

Grease your pan with unscented coconut butter. Next form an even layer on the bottom of your pan with one portion of the batter. Top with ⅓ of the whipped cream, and spread it into an even layer. Set in fridge 20 to 30 minutes until firm. When firm, top evenly with half of the chopped strawberries. Pat together the second layer of cake and lay in place. Again top with ⅓ of the whipped cream, and spread it into an even layer. Set in fridge 20–30 minutes until firm. When firm, top evenly with remainder of your chopped strawberries. Pat together the third and final layer of the cake and lay in place. Set in the fridge for 15 minutes.

Remove the cake from the pan by sliding a thin paring knife around its edge; press the bottom of the pan up and out. Then top with remaining whipped cream and decorate with whole or sliced strawberries.

I Am Assured

GERMAN CHOCOLATE CAKE

Makes one 9-inch cake (you will need a pan with a removable bottom)

FOR THE CAKE

9 cups nut milk pulp (see page 93)
2 cups well packed, very finely chopped dates
¾ cup raw unscented coconut butter
½ cup raw cacao powder
¼ cup vanilla
¼ cup fresh coconut milk (see page 91)
½ teaspoon salt

FOR THE FILLING

5 cups pecans or walnuts
3 cups coconut flakes
1 cup agave nectar
2 tablespoons vanilla
¼ teaspoon salt

TO MAKE THE FILLING

In the bowl of your food processor fitted with the "S" blade, process 4 cups of the nuts with agave, vanilla, and salt until mixture reaches a nut-butter consistency. Transfer to bowl. Add remaining walnuts and the coconut flakes, and mix well.

TO MAKE THE CAKE

Place the chopped dates in the bowl of your food processor fitted with the "S" blade. Process until the dates have reached a smooth paste. This may require adding a little water and scraping down the bowl several times. Next, in a standing mixer with the flat paddle or with a hand mixer at low speed, beat the date, coconut butter, cacao powder, vanilla, coconut milk, and salt until smooth. Add flour and mix at a higher speed until well incorporated. When ready, remove from mixer and separate into two equal portions.

Grease your pan with unscented coconut butter. Form an even layer on the bottom of your pan with half of the batter. Top with half the filling. Pat together the second layer of cake and lay in place. Top with remaining filling. Set in fridge for 30 minutes. Remove the cake from the pan by sliding a thin paring knife around its edge, then press the bottom of the pan up and out. Place the cake on a plate and pour over **I Am Decadent** Raw Chocolate Sauce (see page 148).

> **Note:** For traditional German Chocolate Cake, make additional filling to frost top of cake, omitting **I Am Decadent.**

I Am Magnificent

RAW CHOCOLATE MOUSSE

Serves 5–6

½ ounce Irish moss (see page 151)

½ cup water

2 cups almond milk (see page 92)

¼ cup well packed, finely chopped dates

⅓ cup agave nectar

¼ cup + 2 tablespoons cacao powder (or more for a darker cacao mousse)

2 teaspoons vanilla

⅛ teaspoon salt

2 tablespoons lecithin

½ cup raw unscented coconut butter

With what daily ritual do you celebrate yourself?

Put Irish moss, cut into small pieces, into blender carafe with water and blend on high speed until dissolved and smooth and very thick. Add milk, date, agave nectar, vanilla, salt, and cacao powder and blend until smooth. Add lecithin and coconut butter until well incorporated. Pour into cups and place in fridge/freezer until set (about a half hour).

Do you practice and trust your inner knowing?

I Am Cherished

CASHEW LEMON CHEESECAKE

Makes a 9½-inch cheesecake

FOR THE CRUST
2 cups almonds
¼ teaspoon vanilla
⅛ teaspoon salt
A heaping ¼ cup chopped dates

FOR THE FILLING
3 cups soaked cashews
1½ cups almond milk (see page 92)
1 cup lemon juice
¾ cup agave nectar
1 teaspoon vanilla
2 pinches salt
3 tablespoons lecithin
¾ cup raw unscented coconut butter

GARNISH
Top with lemon zest/slices or fruit of your choice.

TO MAKE THE CRUST

In the bowl of a food processor fitted with the "S" blade, process almonds, vanilla, and salt until finely crumbled. Continue processing while adding small amounts of the dates until crust sticks together. Press crust onto bottom of greased (with raw unscented coconut butter) 9½-inch springform pan.

TO MAKE THE FILLING

Blend all ingredients except lecithin and coconut butter until smooth. Add lecithin and coconut butter and blend until well incorporated. Pour into the springform pan with prepared crust and set in fridge/freezer (about an hour) until firm.

What do you care about?

Note: You can make different-flavored cheesecake by using blended fresh fruit in place of the milk (see photograph on page 115).

I Am Inviting

BANANA CREAM PIE

Makes one 9-inch pie

FOR THE CRUST
⅓ cup well-packed, finely chopped dates
2½ cups coconut flakes
⅛ teaspoon salt
¼ teaspoon vanilla (optional)

FOR THE FILLING
1 cup coconut milk (see page 91)
¼ cup well-packed, chopped dates
3 ripe medium bananas
½ teaspoon salt
1 teaspoon vanilla
½ tablespoon lemon juice
Pinch of turmeric for color
2 tablespoons lecithin
½ cup raw unscented coconut butter

FOR THE COCONUT CREAM TOPPING
¾ cup coconut milk
¼ cup coconut meat (wet measured; see page 124)
¼ cup agave nectar
⅛ teaspoon salt
1 tablespoon vanilla
1 teaspoon lecithin
¼ cup raw unscented coconut butter

TO MAKE THE CRUST

Put coconut flakes, salt, and vanilla in your food processor, fitted with the "S" blade. Begin to process, adding small amounts of the date until crust sticks together. Press crust into a greased (with coconut butter) 9-inch pie pan.

TO MAKE THE FILLING

Blend all ingredients, except the coconut butter and lecithin, until smooth. Blend in the coconut butter and lecithin until smooth. Pour into pie shell and set in freezer or refrigerator until firm (about an hour).

TO MAKE THE COCONUT CREAM TOPPING

Pour coconut milk into blender. Add coconut meat until level reaches one cup, wet measured (meaning that you add the meat until the liquid in the blender reaches the 1-cup level). Next blend remaining ingredients, except lecithin and coconut butter, until smooth. Then add lecithin and coconut butter and blend until incorporated. Set in freezer or refrigerator until firm, and then spoon onto firm pie base.

— ❀ —

Are you willing
to stand for another's
life without their
consent?

I Am Home

APPLE PIE

Makes one 9-inch pie. Note that this wonderful pie
requires dehydration and takes about 12 hours to complete.

FOR THE CRUST
2¾ cups macadamia nuts
⅛ teaspoon salt

FOR THE FILLING

STEP 1
7 medium-sized apples
Splash of lemon juice

STEP 2
½ cup apple juice

STEP 3
1½ cups apple juice
1 ounce Irish moss (see page 151)
⅓ cup well-packed, chopped dates
1 tablespoon yacon syrup (see page 156)
¼ teaspoon cinnamon
⅛ teaspoon salt
½ teaspoon vanilla

FOR THE TOPPING
2 cups walnuts
⅛ cup well-packed, chopped dates
1 teaspoon vanilla
⅛ teaspoon salt

— ❁ —

Can you embrace
all of yourself?

TO MAKE THE CRUST

Blend in food processor until mealy, scraping down sides periodically. Consistency should be smooth, slightly oily, and able to hold when pressed into a ball. Over-processing can result in the excess release of oil.

TO MAKE THE FILLING

Step 1: Core and slice apples to about ¼-inch thickness. Toss with lemon and ginger juice. Spread apples on dehydrator sheet in a single layer. Dehydrate apples at 145° for 1 hour and then at 115° for another 10 hours.

Step 2: Re-hydrate the apples in apple juice by soaking for approximately 30 minutes or until soft. Strain the apples and reserve 1½ cups of the remaining apple juice.

Step 3: Blend the Irish moss with 1 cup of the liquid until smooth, warm, and thick. Scraping down sides occasionally, blend until mixture is uniform and no Irish moss chunks remain. Add the remaining ingredients, again blending until smooth, thick, and slightly warm. Toss this mixture with the dehydrated apples until all apples are coated. Pour apples into pie shell and set in refrigerator until firm.

TO MAKE THE TOPPING

Blend all ingredients in a food processor fitted with the "S" blade until crumbly. Sprinkle over the pie filling once set.

Walnuts are a great source of vitamin A, vitamin E, copper, magnesium, and alpha-linoleic acid, which is a heart protective. Walnuts also contain ellagic acid, an anti-carcinogen, anti-oxidant found in pomegranates.

I Am Perfect

PECAN PIE

Makes one 9-inch pie

FOR THE CRUST
2¾ cups macadamia nuts
⅛ teaspoon salt

FOR THE FILLING
1½ ounces Irish moss (see page 151)
½ cup water
¾ cup agave nectar
1 cup pecans
1¼ cups well-packed, finely chopped dates
2 tablespoons vanilla
1 tablespoon yacon syrup (see page 156)
⅛ teaspoon salt

FOR THE TOPPING
1 cup pecans

TO MAKE THE CRUST

In the bowl of your food processor fitted with the "S" blade, process the macadamia nuts and salt to a dough-like consistency. (Do not over-process or the macadamias will release too much oil.) Press into a 9-inch pie pan.

TO MAKE THE FILLING

Blend Irish moss with water and agave until smooth. Set aside. In the bowl of your food processor fitted with the "S" blade, process pecans until a paste-like consistency is achieved. To this add your blended ingredients, as well as the vanilla, yacon syrup, and salt; process again until smooth. While processing add the chopped date in small amounts until smooth. Spoon mixture into prepared crust. Top with pecans. Chill in fridge for 10–15 minutes.

Does it make any
sense to judge your
creator's creation?

I Am Creative

PUMPKIN PIE

Makes one 9-inch pie

FOR THE CRUST
2½ cups pecans
¼ cup well-packed, finely chopped dates
¼ teaspoon vanilla
⅛ teaspoon salt

FOR THE FILLING
3 cups butternut squash (shredded and medium-packed)
1½ cups coconut milk (see page 91)
¼ cup + 2 tablespoons agave nectar
1 tablespoon vanilla
2 pinches salt
2 teaspoons ginger powder
2 teaspoons cinnamon
½ teaspoon nutmeg
⅛ teaspoon clove
Pinch of turmeric
2 tablespoons lecithin
½ cup + 2 tablespoons raw unscented coconut butter

GARNISH
½ cup pecans

TO MAKE THE CRUST

In the bowl of your food processor fitted with the "S" blade, process pecans, vanilla, and salt briefly. Continue processing while adding small amounts of the date until crust sticks together. Press crust into a greased (with unscented coconut oil) 9-inch pie pan.

You are the artist of your life—what are you painting?

Blend all ingredients except lecithin and coconut butter until smooth. Then add lecithin and coconut butter, blending until well incorporated. Pour into prepared crust and set in fridge/freezer (about 30–45 minutes). Once set, decorate with pecans.

I Am Lovely

STRAWBERRY APPLE COBBLER

Makes a pan 12 x 10 x 2½ inches

FOR THE CRUST
4½ cups pecans (do not soak)
3 tablespoons well-packed, very finely chopped dates
2 tablespoons cinnamon
1 tablespoon vanilla
⅛ teaspoon salt

FOR THE FILLING
8 cups sliced apples
5 cups sliced strawberries
¼ cup lemon
1 tablespoon vanilla
Pinch of salt

TO MAKE THE CRUST

In the bowl of your food processor fitted with the "S" blade, process for 1 minute 3 cups of the pecans with the cinnamon, vanilla, and salt. Continue to process while adding small amounts of the date. Then place in a bowl and add remaining 1½ cups pecans. Press the crust into your pan, setting aside 1½ cups of this crust mixture for the topping.

TO MAKE THE FILLING

Combine all the ingredients in a bowl and mix well. Evenly distribute the filling on top of the crust. Then crumble the remaining crust on the top. This dessert is lovely served with **I Am Pleased** Vanilla Hazelnut Ice Cream (see page 145) or topped with **I Am Smooth** Sweetened Crème Fresh (see page 143).

> **Note:** You may substitute local ripe seasonal fruits for the strawberries and apples.

— ❀ —

How do you move
from your head to
your heart?

I Am Devoted

LIVE COCONUT CREAM PIE

Makes one 9-inch pie

FOR THE CRUST
2½ cups dry coconut flakes
¼ teaspoon vanilla
⅛ teaspoon salt
Heaping ¼ cup well-packed, finely chopped dates

FOR THE FILLING
1¼ cups coconut milk (see page 91)
¾ cup coconut meat (see page 91)
Heaping ¾ cup well-packed, finely chopped dates
½ teaspoon vanilla
2 pinches of salt
3 tablespoons lecithin
½ cup + 2 tablespoons raw scented coconut butter

GARNISH
¾ cup dry coconut flakes

What do you give your life to?

TO MAKE THE CRUST

Put coconut flakes, salt, and vanilla in your food processor, fitted with the "S" blade. Begin to process, adding small amounts of the date until crust sticks together. Press crust into a greased (with coconut butter) 9-inch pie pan.

TO MAKE THE FILLING

Blend coconut milk, meat, date, vanilla, and salt until smooth. Add lecithin and coconut butter and blend until well incorporated. Pour into prepared crust. Set in fridge/freezer until set (about 1 hour). Top with thin layer of coconut flakes. Now you can share your devotion.

I Am Adoring

TIRAMISU

Makes a square pan 8 x 8 x 3 inches

FOR THE CAKE
1⅓ cups well-packed, finely chopped dates
½ cup coconut butter
½ teaspoon salt
2 tablespoons vanilla
30 ounces almond flour
8 ounces cold-processed espresso (see page 114)

FOR THE CACAO MOUSSE
½ ounce Irish moss (see page 151)
1½ cups almond milk (see page 92)
¼ cup + 1 teaspoon well-packed, finely chopped dates
¼ cup agave nectar
2 tablespoons vanilla
⅛ teaspoon salt
⅓ cup cacao powder
1 tablespoon lecithin
Scant ½ cup raw unscented coconut butter

FOR THE WHIPPED CREAM
2¼ cups coconut milk (see page 91)
1½ cups soaked cashews (see page 153)
½ cup + 2 tablespoons agave nectar
2 tablespoons vanilla
⅛ teaspoon salt
2 tablespoons lecithin
⅔ cup raw unscented coconut butter

GARNISH
¼ cup cacao powder

Say three times out loud, "I am adoring myself, I am adoring everyone else, I am the adoring love of God radiating for myself and all."

TO MAKE THE CAKE

First purée the dates in a food processor. To create a fine paste, you may need to add a little water. In a mixer with flat paddle at low speed, mix date, coconut butter, vanilla, and salt until smooth. Add flour and mix at higher speed until well incorporated. Remove from mixer and separate into two equal portions. Grease pan (with unscented coconut butter) and form an even layer on bottom of the pan with one portion. Soak this layer with half of the espresso (4 ounces). Allow espresso to soak in.

TO MAKE THE MOUSSE

Blend Irish moss with ½ cup of milk until dissolved, smooth, and thick. Add remaining milk, date, agave, vanilla, salt, and cacao powder, and blend until smooth. Add lecithin and coconut butter until well incorporated. Pour onto the cake layer. Set in fridge/freezer (about an hour). Once set, layer the other cake portion on top of the mousse and soak cake with remaining espresso. Return to fridge/freezer until ready to top with whipped cream.

TO MAKE THE WHIPPED CREAM

Blend all ingredients except lecithin and coconut butter until smooth. Then add lecithin and coconut butter, blending until well incorporated. Pour onto cake and set in fridge/freezer (about an hour). Once set, dust with cacao powder in an even layer.

I Am Amazing

LEMON MERINGUE PIE

Makes one 9-inch pie

FOR THE CRUST
2¾ cups macadamia nuts
⅛ teaspoon salt

FOR THE FILLING
2¼ ounces Irish moss (see page 151)
1½ cups lemon juice
¾ cup agave nectar
Pinch of turmeric

GARNISH
Use a half recipe of **I Am The Top** Our Live Meringue
(see page 142).

TO MAKE THE CRUST

In the bowl of your food processor fitted with the "S" blade, process
the macadamia nuts and salt to a dough-like consistency (do not over-
process or the macadamias will release too much oil). Press into a
9-inch pie pan.

What fact about
nature inspires you?

Blend Irish moss with lemon juice and turmeric until smooth and thick. Add agave and continue blending until well incorporated. Pour into prepared crust and set in fridge for 20–30 minutes. Top with **I Am The Top** Our Live Meringue (see page 142).

Irish moss acts as a detoxifier and as a treatment for chronic lung disease. Irish moss contains a lot of vitamin A, calcium, iodine, and other minerals.

I Am Bliss

HAZELNUT CHOCOLATE CREAM PIE

Makes one 9-inch pie

FOR THE CRUST
1 cup hazelnuts
1 cup macadamia nuts
¼ teaspoon vanilla
⅛ teaspoon salt
2½ ounces finely chopped dates

FOR THE FILLING
½ ounce Irish moss
1½ cups hazelnut milk*
¼ cup agave nectar
¼ cup well-packed, finely chopped dates
⅓ cup cacao powder
2 teaspoons vanilla
⅛ teaspoon salt
1 Tablespoon + 1 teaspoon lecithin
¼ cup + 2 tablespoons unscented coconut butter

GARNISH
Use ½ recipe of **I Am The Top** Our Live Meringue (see page 142)

Consider that a leader always apologizes first and takes 100% responsibility. Where in your life can you take the lead?

TO MAKE THE CRUST

In the bowl of your food processor fitted with the "S" blade, process hazelnuts, macadamia nuts, vanilla, and salt until crumbly. Continue processing while adding small amounts of the date until crust sticks together. Press the crust into a greased (with unscented coconut oil) 9-inch pie pan.

TO MAKE THE FILLING

Blend Irish moss with ½ cup of the hazelnut milk until smooth and thick. Add remaining hazelnut milk, agave, date, vanilla, salt, and cacao powder. Blend until smooth. Add lecithin and coconut butter, blending until well incorporated. Pour into prepared crust. Place in fridge/freezer until set (about an hour). When set, top pie with a thin layer of meringue. Decorate with cacao nibs and hazelnuts.

*TO MAKE HAZELNUT MILK

In your blender liquefy ¾ cup hazelnuts with 1½ cups water. Blend 1–2 minutes. Let steep 5–10 minutes then strain using a nut milk bag. Yields 1½ cups milk.

I Am Heavenly

MUDSLIDE PIE

Makes one 9-inch pie

FOR THE CRUST
1½ cups coconut flakes
¾ cup almonds
1½ ounces cacao powder
Scant ½ cup well-packed, finely chopped dates
⅛ teaspoon salt
2 teaspoons vanilla

FOR THE WHITE CHOCOLATE FILLING
1¼ cups coconut milk (see page 91)
1¼ cups soaked cashews (see page 153)
¼ cup + 1 tablespoon agave nectar
2 tablespoons vanilla
1 tablespoon + 1 teaspoon lecithin
¼ cup + 1 tablespoon cacao butter

FOR THE ALMOND BUTTER FILLING
⅓ cup raw almond butter
Scant 1¼ cups white chocolate filling

CHOCOLATE FILLING

¼ cup almond milk (see page 92)

2 tablespoons agave nectar

1½ tablespoons cacao powder

1 tablespoon vanilla

Small pinch of salt

1 teaspoon lecithin

2 tablespoons raw cacao butter

TO MAKE THE CRUST

In the bowl of your food processor fitted with the "S" blade, process coconut flakes, almonds, cacao powder, vanilla, and salt until small and crumbly. Continue processing while adding small amounts of the dates until crust sticks together. Press crust into greased (with unscented raw coconut butter) 9-inch pie pan.

TO MAKE THE WHITE CHOCOLATE AND ALMOND BUTTER FILLINGS

Blend all white chocolate filling ingredients except lecithin and cacao butter until smooth. Add lecithin and cacao butter, blending until well incorporated. Leave a little less than 1¼ cups of this mixture in your blender; set the other portion in the fridge/freezer. Add the almond butter to the blender and refrigerate this portion as well.

TO MAKE THE CHOCOLATE FILLING

Blend all ingredients except the lecithin and cacao butter until smooth. Add lecithin and cacao butter, blending until well incorporated. Set in fridge/freezer for 10–15 minutes.

SWIRLING THE FILLINGS

All three fillings must be set to the same consistency—that of loose pancake batter. If any of the fillings have set too far, melt down over a hot water bath, stir, and check frequently until desired consistency is achieved. Spoon the fillings into the prepared crust. Do this in two layers, alternating fillings/colors. With a chopstick inserted almost to the crust, swirl and dance the stick to create a marbled effect. Set in fridge/freezer (about 30–40 minutes) until firm.

I Am Awakening

KEY LIME PIE

Makes one 9-inch pie

If heaven is a choice now, what do you choose?

FOR THE CRUST

1¼ cups macadamia nuts

1¼ cups pecans

Scant ¼ cup well-packed, finely chopped dates

¼ teaspoon vanilla

⅛ teaspoon salt

FOR THE FILLING

¾ cup lime juice

7½ ounces avocado

½ cup + 1 tablespoon agave nectar

¼ cup + 2 tablespoons coconut milk (see page 91)

½ teaspoon vanilla

⅛ teaspoon salt

2 tablespoons lecithin

½ cup + 1 tablespoon raw unscented coconut butter

½ teaspoon Vitamineralgreen (optional; see page 155)

GARNISH

Use a half recipe of **I Am The Top** Our Live Meringue
  (see page 142)

1 lime

TO MAKE THE CRUST

In the bowl of your food processor fitted with the "S" blade, process pecans, macadamia nuts, vanilla, and salt until small and crumbly.

Continue processing while adding small amounts of the chopped dates until crust sticks together. Press crust into greased (with raw unscented coconut butter) 9-inch pie pan.

TO MAKE THE FILLING

Blend all ingredients except lecithin and coconut butter until smooth. Add lecithin and coconut butter, blending until well incorporated. Pour into prepared crust and set in fridge/freezer (for about an hour) until firm. Once set, spread a thin layer of meringue on top and decorate with lime slices.

How is a parking
ticket an awakening?

I Am The Top

OUR LIVE MERINGUE

Makes 2½ cups

¾ ounce Irish moss (see page 151)
½ cup water
1 cup coconut milk (see page 91)
½ cup coconut meat (see page 91)
½ cup soaked cashews (see page 153)
¼ cup + 1 tablespoon agave nectar
1 teaspoon lemon juice
1 teaspoon vanilla
Pinch of salt
1½ teaspoons lecithin
½ cup coconut butter

Blend Irish moss and water until smooth and thick. Add coconut milk, meat, cashews, agave, lemon juice, vanilla, and salt. Blend until smooth. Add lecithin and coconut butter until well incorporated. Pour into a wide, shallow pan and set in fridge for up to 3 hours. When set, top pie; and if you like, peak with the back of a spoon.

— ❀ —

What aspect of your
humanity have you
failed to embrace?
Can you embrace it
now?

ateful

I Am Smooth

Sweetened Crème Fraiche

Makes about 1⅔ cups

1½ cups soaked cashews
1 tablespoon + 2 teaspoons lemon juice
Pinch of salt
3 tablespoons + 1 teaspoon Succanat
½ cup fresh water

Rinse your soaked cashews and place them along with all other ingredients into your blender. Begin to pulse slowly, and then turn up the speed. Add water as necessary to keep your mixture pulling down into the bottom of the blender.

Crème Fraiche is a delicious topping on fruit salad or cobbler.

— ❧ —

Does avoidance of
conflict cost you
your power?

I Am Pleased:
Nut Milk Ice Creams

These vegan ice creams will please even those on a dairy-free diet.

What pleases you
about being human?

Vanilla Hazelnut Ice Cream

Makes 1 quart

1 cup soaked almonds (see page 153)
1 cup hazelnuts
4 cups fresh water
½ cup packed pitted dates
2 tablespoons lecithin
½ teaspoon salt
1 teaspoon vanilla extract or 1 inch of vanilla bean

Rinse and drain the almonds. In the carafe of your blender, place almonds and hazelnuts and the 4 cups fresh water. Blend on high for a few minutes. Don't let the milk get too hot while blending. Strain milk through a milk bag or cheesecloth. Rinse the blender and return the milk along with the dates, lecithin, vanilla, and salt to the blender. Blend well and freeze in your ice cream freezer.

This mix can be kept in your fridge until ready to use and will freeze faster when cold.

Add seasonal berries, fruit, chocolate chips, peppermint, or anything else your heart desires to this homemade ice cream for a real treat. You can also make a sundae using **I Am The Best** Caramel Sauce (see page 147).

Butter Pecan Ice Cream

Makes 1 quart

2 cups pecans
4 cups fresh water
¾ cup packed pitted dates
2 tablespoons lecithin
½ teaspoon salt
1 teaspoon vanilla extract or 1 inch of vanilla bean

Place all the ingredients in the blender and blend on high for a few minutes. Don't let the mixture get too hot while blending. Freeze when ready.

This mix can be kept in your fridge until ready to use and will freeze faster when cold.

This ice cream is sweet and has more body, as it is not necessary to strain pecan milk.

Chocolate Brazil Nut Ice Cream

Makes 1 quart

2 cups Brazil nuts
4 cups fresh water
¾ cup packed pitted dates
2 tablespoons lecithin
½ teaspoon salt
1 teaspoon vanilla extract or 1 inch of vanilla bean
6 tablespoons raw chocolate powder

In the carafe of your blender, place Brazil nuts and the 4 cups fresh water. Blend on high for a few minutes. Don't let the milk get too hot while blending. Strain milk through a milk bag or cheesecloth. Reserve pulp for cake recipes.

Rinse the blender and return the milk along with the dates, lecithin, vanilla, salt, and chocolate powder to the blender. Blend well and freeze.

This mix can be kept in your fridge until ready to use and will freeze faster when cold.

This is a rich chocolate ice cream.

I Am The Best

CARAMEL SAUCE

Makes 1⅓ cups

1 cup macadamia nuts (plus a few chopped
   to add at the end)
½ teaspoon salt
¼ cup almond milk (see page 92)
½ cup raw agave nectar
¼ teaspoon vanilla
½–1 teaspoon yacon syrup

Place all ingredients apart from the yacon syrup in blender. Pulse or start on low and gradually increase the speed until you have achieved a smooth texture. (You may need to add a little more almond milk.)

Now blend in ½ teaspoon yacon syrup, slowly. Taste and add a little more yacon syrup if you like.

Note: If you add too much yacon syrup, the color will change from golden to green!

This sauce is wonderful as an ice cream topping or drizzled on **I Am Thrilled** Cinnamon Rolls (see page 112).

What makes
something the best?

I Am Decadent

RAW CHOCOLATE SAUCE

Makes 2 cups

1½ cups almond milk (see page 92)
¾ cup cacao beans
¾ cup agave nectar
3 tablespoons vanilla
¼ teaspoon salt

Blend all ingredients until smooth, about 3–5 minutes. This is a rich raw chocolate sauce.

— ❀ —

What part of yourself
do you judge,
thereby dividing
yourself?

I Am The Basics
Ingredient Guide

Oh, the basics!

Always buy the best products you can find. After all, they're going into your body. Buying decisions will affect the planet for generations to come. Think of all your purchases as votes. When you buy, you vote for what you want to see and support in the world. For ingredients that may be new or uncommon to you, we list places to source these products in our resource guide, **I Am Resourceful.**

Farmer's markets are a great place to spend your money. I truly believe in organic farming. Though not all farmers can afford the organic certification, talk to the people at your local markets. Lots of farmers don't spray, and smaller farms tend to practice less on a monoculture basis. Think local; join a CSA group to get your produce (community-supported agriculture).

You can grow your own food or at least some of it. Read a book on permaculture. People are growing 10–20% of their own food on their balconies. Think outside the box. In fact, bust it wide open!

Agave Nectar
Extracted from the pineapple-shaped core of a cactus-like plant native to Mexico, agave nectar is best known for its use in making tequila. However, raw agave syrup has a low glycemic level and is absorbed slowly into the body, decreasing the highs and lows associated with sugar intake.

Burdock
A favorite in Japanese cooking, burdock root has a sweet, earthy flavor. The taproot of this magnificent plant is used as a food crop and is incredibly easy to grow. Burdock has many health benefits as a diuretic, diaphoretic, and blood purifier. Its oil is also used to maintain healthy

hair and scalp, reducing itching, redness, and dandruff. Find it at your local heath food store or at Asian markets.

Cacao (raw)

I'll be brief here, as volumes can and have been written on this most blissful of foods. Although not all cacao is roasted, it is all fermented, thus reducing its bitterness. Full of antioxidants and phenyl ethyl-amine—the chemical found in the brains of people in love—it's no wonder people all over the world are attracted to chocolate. Chocolate fruit looks somewhat similar to a small papaya. It's the beans on the inside of the pod that we ferment and use in confections, potions, and brews. Cacao is available in whole beans, nibs, and powder as well as cacao butter, the extracted fat solids.

Chipotle Chile

Chipotle chiles are red ripe jalapeños, dried and smoked, rich in flavor and full of heat. Because chipotles are smoked, technically they aren't raw but are well worth the exception. They can be bought whole or ground.

Coconut Oil

There are two types of coconut oil that we use in the Café, unscented and scented. Using scented coconut oil, sometimes referred to as coconut *butter*, will most definitely impart a rich coconut flavor. Most likely you'll want to have your pantry stocked with both.

———— ❀ ————

"Enthusiasm changes the
quality of the job
because it changes people."

–Norman V. Peale

Daikon Radish

A wonderfully flavorful root vegetable anywhere from 5 to 20 inches long and 2 to 4 inches around, and typically white, daikon is great in salads and crudités and wonderful for making veggie noodles. Daikon is rich in vitamin C, potassium, and folate as well as magnesium. You can find daikon radish at your local farmer's market, heath food store, or Asian market.

E3Live

E3Live is a fresh-frozen blue green algae from Klamath Lake that contains 64 nutrients that are 97% absorbable. It is an anti-inflammatory, powerful detoxifier, and energy and mental clarity booster.

Flax Meal

You can buy flax meal or make some of your own—it's so easy. To make flax meal put a cup or so of flax seeds into your blender and whiz away. Keep any extra in the freezer until you are ready to use it.

Herbs and Spices (dried)

Always buy these organic, as most commercial spices these days are irradiated. Most are available in the bulk section of your local health food store, or check our resource guide for an online source.

Irish Moss

Irish moss is seaweed currently harvested off the island of Jamaica. At the Café, we use it to thicken and bind desserts and cheeses. Rinse irish moss well in cool water and soak 12–24 hours before using in recipe.

Irish moss

Kaffir Lime Leaves

These wonderfully glossy, bright green leaves are used in many dishes from Southeast Asia. They add a citrus tang and floral aroma not to be missed. Kaffir lime trees are very easy to grow in a large pot in virtually any climate. (They may need to come inside in the winter!) To use these leaves, remove the inner vein (which is bitter).

Stack the leaves and cut in fine thin strips (chiffonade). You can usually find these in larger health food stores and Asian markets; they can also be ordered on the Internet. The leaves freeze well, but dried leaves should always be avoided, as the flavor of fresh or frozen is unequalled. If you can't find them or don't want to mail-order them, lime zest is the closest substitute.

Lecithin

At the Café, we use lecithin as an emulsifier in some of our desserts. It helps to bind liquids with oils. We use an organic non-GMO (genetically modified organism) soy lecithin powder. When buying a lecithin, always find one that is non-GMO; soy is traditionally the subject of a great deal of genetic modification. Lecithin protects cells from oxidation, is composed mostly of B vitamins, and breaks down stored fats in our body.

Lemongrass

Lemongrass is a lovely aromatic herb used in the cuisines of Southeast Asia. To use this wonderful herb, cut the lower portion off just above its widest point, and cut the top third off. You'll be left with the tender middle section. Remove its outer leaf (these parts can be used to make a wonderful tea or can be discarded). Now with your sharpest knife, cut across as fine as possible into very thin disks. These disks can be used as is or pounded in a mortar and pestle for a sauce or curry, or blended into a soup.

Olive Oil

At the Café, we use only Bariani stone-crushed organic olive oil, a wonderful artisan olive oil processed at truly low temperatures to ensure a raw and extraordinary product.

Maca Root

Maca grows high in the mountains of Peru. Rich in mineral content, maca is a natural hormone balancer for both men and women. Not only popular for enhancing sexual libido and easing unpleasant menopause symptoms, maca greatly affects energy, stamina, depression, and memory.

Miso

Always use a miso that is un-pasteurized, organic, and GMO-free. In this book we use only mellow white and red misos. Available in many varieties, miso comes from a rich culinary tradition more than a thousand years old; some varieties are not so suited to the Western palate, such as the infamous natto miso. Miso is also very easy to make. One only needs patience to make it, as most misos need to ferment for a minimum of three months for mellow miso and one year for heartier miso. Miso paste is available at your local health food store.

Nama Shoyu

"Nama" means raw or un-pasteurized in Japanese. Full of enzymes and lactobacillus, this is by far the best soy sauce on the market. Don't skimp—you must use this product! For a wheat-free product, use wheat-free Tamari.

Nut Butters

Not all raw nut butters are really raw, even though they might not have been roasted. During processing there is a great amount of friction, and with great amounts of friction come great amounts of heat. To ensure a raw product you need special equipment and a company dedicated to producing really raw products. Check our resource guide for brands and places to find really raw nut butters.

Nuts and Seeds

It's important to buy raw organic nuts and seeds, as toxins are stored in fats. Cashews are one of the harder nuts to find really raw. Typically in processing and removing the skins they are steamed, but really raw cashews are hand-peeled. We share with you an online source in our resource guide.

In most cases it's important to soak seeds and nuts. This will start the sprouting process and make their full nutritional potential available. Soaking will also remove enzyme inhibitors. You don't need to soak Brazil or hazelnuts, as they contain no enzyme inhibitors. When soaking buckwheat it may be best to do so in the fridge if you are in a warm climate. And always rinse buckwheat thoroughly, as it becomes very slimy when soaked. Rinse well in strainer until water is clear. There is no need to rinse flax seeds—they soak up the water and become gelatinous—but pour off excess water if there is any. Rinse all other seeds and nuts well before using.

Here is a little guide for soaking seeds and nuts:

almonds, 12 hours
buckwheat, 6 hours
cashews, 8 hours
flax, 8 hours
pecans, 2 hours
pumpkin seeds, 4–6 hours
sesame seeds, 4 hours
sunflower seeds, 4–6 hours
walnuts, 2 hours

Salt

At the Café, we use only Himalayan Crystal Salt, mined from one of the oldest salt deposits on Earth. It has a superior flavor and an unbelievable 84 essential minerals. It is sold in fine and small crystals for grinding at the table, as well as large stones for making solé. This is a solution of fresh water and the stones, used as a mineral supplement to jump-start our body's electrical system. We also make a great virgin margarita with it at the Café called **I Am Sassy.** This salt is well worth the extra expense; this is not the same product as common table salt!

Himalayan Crystal Salt Stones

Sea Vegetables

Rich in flavor and full of nutrients, seaweeds are easy to add to your diet. Dulse and nori can be eaten like snacks. Arame and hijiki can be soaked and thrown into salads or put into your bubbling brew of kim chee. Wakame makes a great salad. One of the specific benefits is a compound called algenic acid, which binds with heavy metals (such as lead, mercury, and radioactive elements like strontium 90) and carries them out of the body (much like the dipiconlinic acid of miso). Seaweeds also nourish the cardiovascular system, improve digestion, help regulate metabolism and glandular and hormonal flows, and calm the nervous system.

Shiitake Mushrooms

Shiitake mushrooms are native to China and have been cultivated for over 1000 years. They have been researched for their medicinal benefits, most notably their anti-tumor properties and immunological benefits, ranging from anti-viral to possible treatments for allergies and arthritis. Shiitake are also one of a few known natural sources of vegan and kosher vitamin D (vitamin D2). They are best and more flavorful when purchased fresh but are also available dried. For the mushroom marinade, slice shiitake thin and toss with ¼ cup lemon juice and ¼ cup Nama Shoyu.

Succanat

Succanat is dehydrated, unprocessed sugar cane juice. Succanat makes a great raw and affordable sweetener with a wonderful light molasses flavor.

Solé

Solé is a saturated Himalayan Crystal Salt solution. Place these salt crystals in a glass jar or canister and fill with filtered water. Keep adding salt crystals until the water can absorb no more and crystals can be seen at the bottom of the jar. This is now a saturated salt solution called solé. See "Salt," above.

Thai Young Coconuts

Young coconuts are a wonder food, more nutritious than whole milk and full of natural sugars, salts, and vitamins. Look for coconuts that have had their green husks shaved into a semi-conical shape. They should only be purchased when almost pure white. (Any nuts that sit on the shelf long enough to turn brown most likely won't be great.) Young coconuts are available at Asian markets, health food stores, and sometimes at larger grocery stores. Unfortunately, they are not available organic. Instructions on opening and extracting the meat and juice are available on page 91.

Vitamineralgreen

Vitamineralgreen is a nutrient-dense superfood containing a full spectrum of naturally occurring absorbable and non-toxic vitamins, minerals, and trace elements. Also naturally occurring are all the essential amino acids, antioxidants, fatty acids, chlorophyll, soluble and insoluble fibers, and a plethora of other synergistically bound, organic nutrients.

Yacon Syrup

Yacon is another superfood of the Andes, a probiotic sweetener that is similar in flavor to molasses. In recipes it is used to add that bottom flavor of caramelized sugar and to contribute a rich warm color as well.

What is one
core belief you
have about life
that you love?

I Am Equipped
Equipment Guide

At the Café's central kitchen where I tested most of these recipes, we have some wonderful and extremely powerful equipment. But just to prove a point, I made all these recipes on standard home equipment. I borrowed an Osterizer 14-speed blender. It held up great and got the job done. (A home blender is not recommended for recipes calling for Irish moss.) Also, I bought a Cuisinart seven-cup food processor, which also worked great. So I say use what you have. If you find yourself doing large batches, or if your blender burns out, go ahead and upgrade. You don't need to buy the most expensive equipment to prepare raw cuisine. You'll be amazed at what you can do with a chef's knife, a grater, and a mortar and pestle. You'll find some of the following in **I Am Resourceful,** our resource guide.

Blenders
Most home blenders will get the job done. If you're going high-tech, purchase a Vitamix or K-Tech Blender. It's always important to use enough liquid when blending. Even the most expensive blender will shut itself off if you try to process too dry of a load. (The only exception is making flax meal, for which you should use no liquid.)

"Every moment is a golden one
for him who has
the vision to recognize it as such."

–Henry Miller

Coffee Grinder

An electric coffee grinder is a great tool to have around for grinding dry spices, making flax meal, and processing cacao (whole and nibs) into powder. You'll want to wipe out the grinder well with a damp cloth between ingredients.

Crocks/Fermentation Vessels

There is a lot of leeway here. You can use anything from food-grade plastic buckets up to beautiful ceramic crocks for making sauerkraut, kim chee, miso, and homemade beer and wine.

Dehydrators

I don't think there is an alternative to the Excalibur dehydrator. They are fan-operated and have a thermostat, which is crucial. If you don't own a dehydrator, the oven with only the pilot light on and the door cracked will work. Or try sun drying. Neither is as easy as the Excalibur but would work fine. You can use Teflex sheets over a sheet pan or wire rack, or lightly oil a sheet pan to make crackers.

Food Processors

If you already own a food processor, use it til it quits. If you're going to purchase a food processor, I highly recommend a Cuisinart. They are great for mixing pâtés as well as quickly grating and slicing vegetables.

Juicers

At the Café, we use a commercial juice press. One side is a grinder, and the other side is a hydraulic press. A juice press for home use is called the Norwalk juicer, and it is almost magical. It yields a higher amount of juice with little or no oxidation, and it produces juice with a higher mineral content. But the price can be a little daunting: about $2,000 for a stainless steel model. So I'd recommend either a Green Star or a Champion.

Knives

Buy the best knives you can afford, and always keep them sharp. When possible, try them out at the store before buying. They should feel comfortable in your hand. Usually all you'll need are a chef's knife, a paring knife, a small-serrated knife, and a cleaver for opening coconuts. Choose knives that are high-carbon stainless steel or ceramic.

Mandolin
This is a great precision tool for slicing and shredding in a snap. Also, it makes short work of julienne vegetables and will also slice paper-thin lasagna noodles.

Nut Milk Bags
These are useful little nylon bags, used in separating nut milk from its pulp. They are great for hanging and draining fresh-made nut cheese. For large batches, paint-straining bags work well and are available at your local hardware store.

Pepper Mills
Freshly ground pepper is unequaled. I have mills for both black and white peppercorns.

Spiralizer
This is a wonderful hand-powered gizmo. It makes veggies into angel hair or fettuccini pasta in the blink of an eye. It is also great for shredding onions and cabbage.

Teflex Sheets
These are Teflon-coated cloths used for dehydrating things that are too liquefied or sticky to place directly on the grid trays.

Wheatgrass Juicers
Hand-crank wheatgrass juicers are very efficient and affordable. I've seen them for $50 to $100 on the Internet.

"The greatest use for life is to spend
it for something that will outlast it."

–Henry James

I Am Technical
Some Helpful Techniques

Using Your Knife

Not everyone has good knife skills; however, with a little patience and practice, good technique can be acquired. Here are a few tips and terms for slicing and dicing. I hope you'll find them useful.

While chopping, use your fingers as a guide. Curl them up with the nails facing the blade. Slide your fingers across the piece of fruit or vegetable as you slice. A chef's knife is shaped so that you can pivot and rock the blade and not have to pick it up after every cut. Remember, round hard vegetables such as carrots are easier to cut if first cut in half lengthwise. This will create a stable flat surface that won't roll while cutting.

Different ways of cutting your food will produce different energies. It's like Yin and Yang. Generally speaking, cutting with the grain of a vegetable brings out the sweet Yin aspect. Cutting against the grain produces the stronger Yang aspect. This is particularly true with onions.

Full Moons, Half Moons, and Quarter Moons

These cuts work well on cylindrical root veggies as well as cucumbers and squash. For full moons, simply slice into disks of the desired thickness. For half moons, first slice the vegetable in half lengthwise. Now lay the two halves cut side down on your board and slice to desired thickness. For quarter moons simply cut the halves lengthwise again before slicing.

Bias Cut

This means cutting on an angle. With practice, this will get easier and more uniform. Aim for about a 45° angle. This is a very beautiful cut, especially on scallions and roots, such as burdock and carrots.

Chiffonade

This cut is most common with basil and other large-leafed herbs. To perform a proper chiffonade, stack the leaves, roll them up, and slice them ⅛ of an inch or thinner. Note: Kaffir lime leaves are very thick and shouldn't be rolled before slicing.

Julienne

A julienne cut is a strip ⅛–¼ inch wide. For hard vegetables such as carrots, first cut on the bias, stack, and then julienne into strips.

Mincing Ginger

To mince ginger that isn't full of unwanted strings and fibers, first scrape away the skin with the edge of a spoon. Wipe off any excess bits of skin and place on your cutting board. With your sharpest knife, cut the ginger into very thin disks (across the grain). Stack the disks and julienne, then gather the julienne ginger and cross-cut very finely. Now you have perfectly minced ginger.

—— ❀ ——

"What is lost shall be found,
though not always
in the same place."

–Janis J. Kinens

I Am Resourceful:

A Source Guide for Equipment, Live Foods, and Education

Resources Available at Café Gratitude

For those of you who live near a Café Gratitude, we carry many of the specialty items used in live-food preparation, and we are getting ready to expand our retail offerings. We currently offer raw cacao, coconut oil, olives, olive oil, Himalayan Crystal Salt, hemp seeds, maca, Vitamineralgreen, E3Live, nut milk bags, goji berries, many cutting-edge nutritional supplements, and a variety of books. We invite you to visit the retail area of our cafés and at www.cafegratitude.com

Many of the ingredients you may be unfamiliar with are available at your local health food store or coop as well as online at both www. essentiallivingfoods.com and www.sunfood.com, two of the largest retail live-food websites.

Fresh Vegetables

Of course, your local farmer's markets and health food stores.

— Robin Van En Center for CSA Resources; online directory of Community-Supported Agriculture farms: www.csacenter.org or call 717.264.4141 x3352

Nuts, Seeds, Flours, and Nut Butters

Your local health food store's bulk section and online at:

— Rejuvenative Foods: www.rejuvenative.com

— Living Tree Organics: www.deliciousorganics.com

— Raw Living Foods: www.eatraw.com or call 866.432.8729

— David Wolfe's Sunfood Nutrition: www.sunfood.com

— Morning Side Farm: www.morningsidefarm.com or call 615.563.2353

Herbs

– Frontier Natural Foods, Organic Bulk Herbs and Spices:
www.frontiercoop.com or call 800.669.3279
– Morning Side Farm: www.morningsidefarm.com or call
615.563.2353

Sea Vegetables

– For Irish Moss: www.cafegratitude.com
– For Sea Vegetables: Mendocino Sea Vegetable Company,
www.seaweed.net

Oils

– Bariani Olive Oil (raw, extra virgin olive oil):
www.barianioliveoil.com or call 415.864.1917

Equipment

Crocks/Fermentation Vessels

– Beautiful earthenware fermentation crocks:
www.wisementrading.com or call 888.891.8411
– Lehman's Hardware; ceramic crocks as well as low-tech
back-to-the-land equipment: www.lehmans.com or call
877.438.5346
– Morning Side Farm; in addition to food-grade plastic buckets
(for fermenting), they operate a monthly organic and natural
bulk food, vitamin, and body care buying club:
www.morningsidefarm.com or call 615.563.2353

Juicers, Dehydrators, and Blenders

Your best bet is to do a Google search and shop for the best price. But
here are a couple of our favorites, particularly for hand-cranked wheatgrass juicers:

– www.discountjuicers.com
– www.livingright.com

Nut Milk Bags

– Elaina Love offers many tools and ingredients that are useful
for a live-food lifestyle, including nut milk bags and Irish
moss: www.purejoyplanet.com

Spiralizers

There seem to be three types of spiral cutters on the market. I find the "turning slicer" that runs about $70 to $100 my favorite, but you can search online for a spiralizer that suits your needs and budget. These are also available at:

- www.sunfood.com
- www.discountjuicers.com
- www.rawgourmet.com

Cold-Process Coffee Brewing System
- Filtron: www.4filtron.com

Food Information and Action
- Genetically Engineered Food Alert: www.gefoodalert.org or call 800.390.3373
- *The Future of Food,* DVD by Lily Films: an in-depth look at genetically modified foods. Available at www.futureoffood.com

Vegan Educational DVDs and Books
- *Earthlings,* narrated by Joaquin Phoenix
- *Food Revolution* by John Robbins
- www.petacatalog.org
- Greenpeace True Food Now Project: www.truefoodnow.org or call 800.326.0950
- Organic Consumers Association: www.organicconsumers.org or call 218.226.4164

Organization for World Food Supply Issues
- Food First-Institute for Food and Development Policies: 398 60th Street, Oakland, California 94618; 510.654.4400, www.foodfirst.com

"I know well what I am fleeing from but not what I am in search of."

—Michel Montaigne

I Am Organized

Index

About the Authors

Terces Engelhart has been preparing and serving flavorful food and delicious meals since her childhood. She is interested in the healing power of food to help people who suffer from diet-based diseases, as she did.

Engelhart and her husband, Matthew, opened the first location of their popular Café Gratitude in 2004 in San Francisco, California. They have opened a second restaurant in San Francisco as well as ones in Berkeley, Marin, and Los Angeles. The cafés, which support local farmers, sustainable agriculture, and environmentally friendly products, serve living, organic food made with the freshest ingredients possible.

The Engelharts published *The Abounding River Personal Logbook* as well as *The Abounding River* board game, both of which focus on their practice of being in abundance. In addition, they lead monthly workshops on this topic and are often asked to be guests on radio and TV shows. The Engelharts live with two of their five children in San Francisco.

Orchid (Richard Slayen) has studied food and cooking in such exotic places as Thailand, Indonesia, Singapore, Australia, Central America, and Mexico. He specializes in creating fabulous meals designed to delight the senses and nourish the body. Orchid currently resides in San Francisco, California, and Liberty, Tennessee, seducing the palates of private clients as well as the community at Café Gratitude.